W9-CYC-372

PRIDE

FOR THE LOVE OF KIRBY, KENT, AND KILLEBREW

ALAN ROSS

Cumberland House
Nashville, Tennessee

TWINS PRIDE
Published by:
CUMBERLAND HOUSE PUBLISHING, INC.
431 Harding Industrial Drive
Nashville, TN 37211-3160

Cover design: Gore Studio, Inc., Nashville, Tennessee
Book design: John Mitchell
Research assistant: Ariel Robinson

Library of Congress Cataloging-in-Publication Data

Twins pride : for the love of Kirby, Kent, and Killebrew / [edited
by] Alan Ross.
    p. cm.
  Includes bibliographical references (p. 247) and index.
  ISBN-13: 978-1-58182-525-1 (pbk. : alk. paper)
  ISBN-10: 1-58182-525-0 (pbk. : alk. paper)
  1. Minnesota Twins (Baseball team)—History—Quotations,
maxims, etc. 2. Washington Senators (Baseball team : 1886-
1960)—History—Quotations, maxims, etc. I. Ross, Alan, 1944-
  GV875.M55T87 2006
  796.357'6409776579—dc22

                    2005036541

Printed in the United States of America

1 2 3 4 5 6 7—12 11 10 09 08 07 06

For Caroline,
love you so

Harmon Killebrew

CONTENTS

INTRODUCTION

It was some time back in the Pre-Pleistocene Era. I was taking in the world through the magic of our black & white TV sitting in my parents' den, enthralled by a show on the television before me. A bevy of baseball's finest sluggers contested each other in a nine-inning game, hitting batting-practice home runs. Anything not a home run was an out. It was the great classic *Home Run Derby*, which ran from 1959 through '61.

On this particular episode, Harmon Killebrew, a young Washington Senator and budding Minnesota Twin, was challenging incumbent winner Mickey Mantle. The Yankee power hitter had won something like five or six straight weeks in a row, accepting challenges from the likes of big hitters Willie Mays, Roy Sievers (another Senator), Al Kaline, and Hank Aaron. But on this occasion, The Mick was more than met by The Killer. Mighty No. 3 took the match, coming from behind in the late innings to defeat Mantle. It was to be my first tangible connection to the future franchise from the North Country.

While the accomplishments recorded in Minnesota have been timeless and thrilling, it has been no less fascinating to revisit the early days of the franchise's history—those inchoative days of the American League when the club was playing in the nation's capital as the Washington Senators. What names! Walter Johnson, "the Big Train"; "the Wild Goose of the Potomac," Goose Goslin; boy-wonder second baseman and manager Bucky Harris. . . . The Senators got to the World Series three times, equaling their modern-day counterparts in the Twin Cities, but the Twins have taken two world-championship crowns (1987 and '91) to Washington's lone Series triumph in 1924.

Heroes abound, with a deluxe cast of star ballplayers through the years that has included the likes of Mickey Vernon, Eddie Yost, Killebrew, Tony Oliva, Rod Carew, Jim Kaat, Jim Perry, Kent Hrbek, Kirby Puckett, Bert Blyleven, Torii Hunter, and Johan Santana.

Twins Pride is the story of the American League's Minnesota franchise, as told by the players themselves, the managers, coaches, opponents, fans, and media. An all-time Twins franchise nine is presented, as well as the complete rosters of all three world-champion Senators/Twins teams, a chapter on the various venues, and even a shrine of superlatives to the greatest Twin of them all—Harmon Killebrew.

From Tovar to the Big Train, Pascual to Puck, Hisle to Hunter, and Versalles to Viola—it's Twins time!

TWINS TRADITION

When they began importing homer hankies into the hospitals to cover the bottoms of newly born babies, I knew Minnesota had made it to the bigs in unglued hysteria.

Jim Klobuchar

author,
prior to the 1987 World Series

On Feb. 1, 1901, Jimmy Manning announced the makeup of the new team that would open the American League season for Washington. . . . With the exception of "Wild Bill" Everitt and Emmett Phyle, who came from Chicago, all had played with Kansas City in 1900. In fact, it was the K.C. team transferred to Washington.

Morris A. Bealle
author

FAST FACT: Manning became the Senators' first manager in the brand-new American League, in 1901, as a gift from AL President Ban Johnson for Manning's agreement to drop his Kansas City franchise out of Johnson's well-established minor circuit, the Western League. Manning wqnted more eastern cities in his new American League mix of teams, so in return, Johnson awarded Manning the new Washington franchise.

Washington—First in War, First in peace, Last in the American League.

Popular phrase in the nation's capital
during the first half of the 20th century

Washington won its American League opener in Philadelphia, 5 to 1. Carrick, by that time re-nicknamed "Poker Bill" because of his inept handling of the cards, held Philadelphia to five hits, three of which were made by Larry Lajoie, one of the great hitters of all time.

Morris A. Bealle

The game itself was a notable one in that it showed the country at large, but especially Washington fans, that the national capital has at last acquired an aggregation of ball tossers who are a credit and not a disgrace.

Washington Post

following the Senators' inaugural game, April 26, 1901, a 5–1 win over Philadelphia

The year 1901 saw the crude start of the present public address system at sporting events. . . . In those days the umpire used to turn around and announce the batteries to the press box in a tone that nobody could hear or understand. E. Lawrence Phillips, who owned the scorecard concession at the Senators' home games, conceived the idea of taking a megaphone out to the bleachers and telling the two-bit customers what was what. Near the end of the season the crowds began to ride the umpires for their farcical announcing. One day [umpire] Tim Hurst asked Phillips if he would pinch hit for him in informing the press box at the start of the game. This was the start of intelligent announcing.

Morris A. Bealle

In spite of his mutilation of the word *batteries*, which he called "batter-eeze," and the extra syllables he often added to players' names, Phillips continued to announce the Washington games until July 4, 1928, being often called on to announce World Series before the mechanical amplifier came into use.

Morris A. Bealle

The past season's experience has convinced me that the team must have hitters to win games.

Washington Star

at the close of the Washington Senators'—and the American League's—debut season in 1901

The 1904 Senators set a record never equaled before nor since by losing the first 13 games of the season.

Morris A. Bealle
1947

The new owners desire to get as far away as possible from the old regime and start the coming season without any barnacles to hinder its move toward prosperity. With that end in view, it is proposed to bury the moss-covered title of Senators and secure a nickname that may be lucky and popular.

Tom Noyes

president of the American League's Washington club, 1905

FAST FACT: The nickname "Senators" had been the appellation of several Washington incarnations prior to the American League entry in 1901, most of them losing teams. Noyes called for a contest among the fans to decide the new team name. The organization received 2,305 suggestions, most favoring "Nationals"—the nickname of the successful 1867 team in Washington. The name was officially annexed to the club. Though called the Senators almost entirely throughout their tenure in the nation's capital, not until 1957, only four years before the franchise relocated to Minnesota, was the club officially renamed the Senators.

The year 1910 was the first time in the history of baseball that a president of the United States opened the season by throwing the first ball. Before 12,028 fans, President Taft performed the honors and saw Walter Johnson beat the Athletics with one hit, 3 to 0. . . . President Taft, in spite of a big bay window, threw the ball with the finesse and grace of an accomplished ball player. He is the only president with such a throwing arm. His successors, Wilson, Harding, Coolidge, Hoover, and Roosevelt, all used the bean-bag stance of a bloomer girl debutante.

Morris A. Bealle

Clark Griffith came to Washington in the spring of 1912 to take over the management of the team, with neither fanfare nor trumpets. Even though he was already known as the "Old Fox of Baseball," his coming excited no ebullient hopes in the breasts of the city's long-suffering and oft disappointed baseball fans. They were used to new managers and old promises. . . . Griffith had been a great old warhorse for the American League, helping organize it in 1900 and incidentally was its leading pitcher in 1901.

He had put a team in New York—the richest major-league territory extant—by raiding National League clubs with the finesse of an expert. . . . He had handled with great skill the reins of the New York Club for six years, coming within an ace of winning the pennant twice. This was in the days when the New Yorkers had no millionaires' checkbooks handy. . . . Within two months after Griffith took charge on the field of actual play, the national capital had a team of which it not only could be proud but which had the whole baseball world agape.

Morris A. Bealle

*They'll tell you there is nothing new
beneath the shining sun.
They'll whisper there is naught to do
that hasn't yet been done.
Which may have been a truthful spiel
some few short weeks ago,
But how about those Senators
with fourteen in a row!*

Grantland Rice

*legendary sports journalist,
during the course of the Senators'
17-game winning streak in 1912*

The Griffiths of the game had faith in the integrity of the sport, confidence in the honesty of players, and the vision of baseball going on to big things.

Bucky Harris

*second base (1919–28)/
manager (1924–28, 1935–42,
1950–54)*

The Griffith family brought to Minnesota a tradition of signing young, talented Cuban players in the pre-Fidel Castro era. One of the best was righthander Camilo Pascual, who won 20 games in 1962 and 21 in 1963, and led the American League in strikeouts in '61, '62 and '63.

Dave Mona
Dave Jarzyna
authors/sports journalists

As free agency became a fact of life and salaries began to rise, baseball became a business different from the one Clark Griffith taught Calvin. And in 1984, believing that the time was right, Calvin decided to sell the club that had been under Griffith ownership for more than 70 years for about $32 million.

Dave Mona
Dave Jarzyna

We certainly don't go into anything that we don't think is going to be fun. . . . Sure, making money is wonderful, but you have to enjoy what you're doing.

Carl R. Pohlad

owner (1984–)

TIMELESS TWINS

Not every player with major-league talent can be a Kent, Kirby, or Kaat; a Carew, Killebrew, or Santana. The everyday working fabric of Twins baseball is supported just as importantly by timely contributions from an Eddie Yost, a Rich Reese, or a Greg Gagne. The rosters are filled with regular heroics from the Lombardozzis, the Smalleys, the Goltzes, and the Boswells . . . vital cogs in the wheel, each with his singular contribution, all in Twinstripes.

From Eddie Yost, the Senators could anticipate the finest third base protection in the league plus the asset of his ability to get on base more than any other lead-off man.

Shirley Povich
sports journalist/author

⚾ ⚾ ⚾

A black Pontiac convertible pulled up to the Twins' Orlando, Florida, training camp in 1961. A man dressed in black Western clothing climbed out of the car. One pearl-handled pistol was holstered on each hip. "Pistol Pete" Ramos, who would become Minnesota's first opening day pitcher, had arrived.

Dean Urdahl
author

⚾ ⚾ ⚾

If I got a win for every ball my outfielders dropped, I'd have been one of the best pitchers in the league.

Pedro Ramos
*pitcher (Wash: 1955–60;
Minn: 1961)*

I'd rather give up a base hit than a base on balls. I wasn't afraid to challenge. Sometimes I win, sometimes I lose. One time I told Mickey Mantle I would only throw him fastballs, my best against him. The first two times up I struck him out; the third time he hit one 600 feet.

Pedro Ramos

FAST FACT: Mantle's gargantuan blast off Ramos in 1954 smashed the right-field upper-deck façade and missed being the first ball ever hit out of Yankee Stadium by just 18 inches.

Every team I went to started dying when I got there. Only the Twins got better.

Pedro Ramos

who played for the Cleveland Indians and New York Yankees when both teams were in decline. They were among the six other teams Ramos pitched for after hurling seven seasons with Washington/Minnesota

Minnesota native Fred Bruckbauer earned a place in baseball trivia books by allowing three hits and a walk while failing to retire a single Washington batter in his one-game major-league career.

Dave Mona
Dave Jarzyna

FAST FACT: Bruckbauer's all-too-brief career with the Twins took place in 1961.

Mudcat Grant had an unusual motion. He would tap the mound with his foot before releasing the ball. His Twins catcher, Earl Battey, laughingly accused him of pitching from 60 feet, not 60 feet, 6 inches, because he gradually moved forward when tapping.

Dean Urdahl

The art of pitching was setting up hitters. Back in those days pitchers had their pitch and hitters had their pitch. . . . The outside corner of the plate was the pitcher's. The other spots were the hitter's. If you didn't pitch inside, the outside corner didn't mean anything because the hitters would go out there and get it.

Jim "Mudcat" Grant
pitcher (1964–67)

The World Series year of 1965 was Grant's big season. He went 21–7, leading the American League in victories, winning percentage, and shutouts (six). He won two games and lost one in the Series against the Dodgers. He helped himself in his 5–1 triumph in Game Six when he jacked a three-run homer.

Dean Urdahl
on Mudcat Grant

I struck out four that inning.

Dave Boswell

*pitcher (1964–70),
on an inning against the New
York Yankees, in which he struck
out Mickey Mantle, but a passed
ball enabled Mantle to safely
reach first. Boswell struck out
the other three New York batters*

Ever since I was nine years old, they knew I could throw a ball better than anyone else my age. I was a honed instrument to be a ballplayer. I wouldn't even marry my wife until I made the big leagues.

Dave Boswell

Outfielder Ted Uhlaender is the only player ever to be chosen the Twins' most improved player for two consecutive seasons (1967, '68).

Jack Clary

author

The year he joined the Twins, 1967, was a big rebound year for Dean Chance. He won the American League Comeback Player of the Year Award. Chance was 20–14 for the Twins and threw two no-hitters. One went five innings, shortened by rain; the other was a 2–1 handcuffing of the Cleveland Indians.

Dean Urdahl

⚾ ⚾ ⚾

Rich Reese hit three pinch-hit grand slams in his career for a major-league record. He still holds the record alone in the American League.

Dean Urdahl

⚾ ⚾ ⚾

Go up there hacking.

Rich Reese

first baseman (1964–73),
his philosophy on hitting

Named the Twins' most valuable player in 1970, Cesar Tovar may be best known for the game he played on Sept. 22, 1968. On that day, Pepe played all nine positions, starting on the mound and working his way through the lineup playing one spot per inning. He led the club to a 2–1 victory over the Oakland A's. On the mound, he blanked the A's and struck out one batter. Now, what self-respecting major-leaguer would allow himself to be struck out by some upstart infielder/outfielder trying to fill up the ballpark with a sideshow gimmick? Reggie Jackson.

Dave Mona
Dave Jarzyna

I tied a major-league record by getting hit three times in one game. I wasn't crowding the plate; it was a left-handed pitcher. He threw a real hard-breaking slider that broke way inside. The first one hit me on my back foot on my toe. The next time up he hit me on my back leg on my shin. The next time on my back leg on my thigh. My only regret is that I didn't get hit a fourth time to set the record.

Craig Kusick
first baseman (1973–79)

I don't care what you hit. I just want you to quell riots on the bench and be ready to play when I put you in on defense.

Billy Martin
manager (1969),
to Frank Quilici, a utility infielder
and defensive replacement for
Martin in 1969

Dave Goltz pitched longer, eight years, than any other Twin without ever having a losing season. That's sometimes a little trivia question I like to throw at people.

Herb Carneal

*longtime Twins broadcaster,
on the Minnesota pitcher from
1972 through '79*

Larry Hisle probably is the most well liked and respected player on the team. You're just not going to find a guy with more class.

Danny Thompson

*shortstop (1970–76),
on the Twins' outfielder from
1973 through '77*

Ron Davis was a very hyper guy on the mound. Once, in Boston, he was so nervous that he didn't wait for a sign from catcher Mark Salas but threw a pitch before Salas had put his mask on.

Herb Carneal

on the Twins' hurler from 1982 through '86

⚾ ⚾ ⚾

Greg Gagne didn't play right away but went on to become the most dependable shortstop the Twins ever had.

Herb Carneal

on the club's shortstop from 1983 through '92

⚾ ⚾ ⚾

Juan Berenguer stalked in with his glowering Pancho Villa moustache and boardinghouse paunch and his late-inning smoke.

Jim Klobuchar

on the Twins' late-'80s closer

Nineteen eighty-seven was special because I was a rookie. Your dream is not only to get to the big leagues, but once you get there, to play in the World Series. I accomplished that in one year.

Gene Larkin

first baseman (1987–93)

⚾ ⚾ ⚾

Scott Erickson was the one pitcher who took tremendous stuff to the mound in the first inning.

Tom Kelly

manager (1986–2001)

⚾ ⚾ ⚾

Randy Bush excelled in the role of pinch hitter. During the Twins' 1991 pennant drive, he had a stretch of seven pinch-hits in a row. . . . Randy tied an American League record with two consecutive pinch-hit home runs in 1986.

Dean Urdahl

He was an incredible athlete. He ran hard, threw hard, and hit hard. Dave Winfield was a visually intimidating force. He was so aggressive. He'd stand at the plate and wave the bat, and it looked small in his hands. . . . He hit extremely hard line drives that went over the fence.

Mike Kingery

10-year major-league outfielder, on the two-year Twins outfielder (1993–94) and future Hall of Famer

Minnesota has played eight straight one-run games, winning the last two on ninth-inning hits by Jacque Jones to take an important three-game series from Baltimore. . . . Jones homered the other way on the first pitch he saw from Jason Grimsley. His infield single Tuesday night gave Minnesota a 4–3 win.

Associated Press

on Jones's game-winning spree July 19 and 20, 2005

He walked a guy in L.A. the other day. I was ready to go to the mound and say, "What are you doing?"

Rick Anderson

pitching coach (2002–),
on a rare walk from Brad Radke,
owner of the best walk percentage
in baseball

FAST FACT: Through mid-June 2005, Radke led all qualifying big-league starters in first-pitch strike percentage, with an over-the-top 77.1 percent (the major-league average is 58.5). As a staff, the Twins hurled more strikes (66.9 percent) than any other team in baseball.

It's hard to believe there could be a pitcher on this planet who averages nearly 100 batters between walks (388 hitters faced, four walks). But Radke is. This man started out the [2005] season by walking one of the first 247 hitters who stepped into the box. Read that stat a few times and digest it.

Jayson Stark

ESPN.com

He's the guy who sets the example for everyone else. [Carlos] Silva just worships Radke. He calls him "the Professor." Silva actually comes out and watches him throw his bullpens. Then he'll come away and say, "The Professor is good." They all watch him. They watch how he attacks the strike zone. If Radke can do that, throwing 88–90 [mph], a guy like Silva, who throws 91–93, says, "Why can't I do that?"

Rick Anderson

His ball moves so much that even if he throws that sinker in the middle of the plate, they still pound it into the ground.

Rick Anderson

on pitcher Carlos Silva

I thought our kid Baker did a super job. He's pretty much given us a chance all season. That's all you can ask.

Ron Gardenhire

manager (2002–),
on 24-year-old rookie pitcher
Scott Baker, who gave up just
two hits and one run in seven
innings in a 2–1 loss to the
Central Division-leading (and
soon-to-be world champion)
Chicago White Sox, Sept. 16,
2005

⚾ ⚾ ⚾

One of the best swings I have ever seen.

Paul Molitor

designated hitter/first base
(1996–98),
on catcher Joe Mauer

⚾ ⚾ ⚾

I don't think I've ever seen a young hitter recognize pitches the way he does.

Scott Ullger

Twins batting coach,
on Joe Mauer

You just signed the next .400 hitter.

Joe Mauer's Grandpa Jake

to Twins GM Terry Ryan

I want to be more like Joe Mauer at the plate.

Torii Hunter

center fielder (1997–)

We had some concern from the start that he was bigger than the normal catcher. But Joe Mauer is not normal, from his mind to his tools to his heart.

Mike Radcliff

Twins scouting director

Joe Nathan became the third Twins pitcher to record 40 saves in consecutive seasons, joining Rick Aguilera (1991–92) and Eddie Guardado (2002–03).

Associated Press

following Nathan's save in a 3–1 win over the Kansas City Royals, Sept. 27, 2005

CHARACTER

Baseball is a lesson in human beings, people's dispositions, and how they handle themselves. You get a good read on people and how they perform under pressure. It helped me in 25 years in business to know how people respond. Baseball was really, truly a life lesson.

Frank Quilici
second baseman (1965, 1967–70)/manager (1972–75)

Self-fear is one of the hardest enemies a man has to conquer, but like most other troubles, it is largely imaginary. Firmly met, it soon vanishes.

Bucky Harris

⚾ ⚾ ⚾

I didn't want the world knowing. I didn't want sympathy. I didn't want to make an error and have people say, "Well, you can't blame him because he has leukemia."

Danny Thompson

⚾ ⚾ ⚾

He brought me over to the side and said, "You know, your dad helped me out; I'm going to help you out. Whatever you need, I'm here for you." Then he smiled. I thought, *This doesn't normally happen in baseball.*

Ken Griffey Jr.
on Kirby Puckett

No one has worked harder this spring than Eric Soderholm. If everyone on the club worked like Eric, we could enter the Twins in the Olympics.

Danny Thompson

on the 1970s Twins third baseman,
a physical fitness devotee

Hey, things may be going bad now but the day we clinch it you're going to be on that mound, and you're going to forget all about the bad days we all went through.

Dan Gladden

outfielder (1987–91),
to teammate and pitcher
Jeff Reardon early in the 1987
season, when the Twins' reliever
was experiencing mound woes.
Reardon was on the hill in the
ninth inning to preserve Minnesota's
AL West crown win over Texas
in late September

We did not become baseball players with the idea of going through 60–102 seasons. We were in it to be winners, and that's what we wanted to work to accomplish. Now that we've done that, it's a great feeling. That's something we can all enjoy together.

Tim Laudner

catcher (1981–89),
who suffered with the atrocious
1982 team before becoming a
world champion in '87

They won, and we can't make any excuses. They didn't make any when they got beat up, and we shouldn't when they beat us.

Gary Gaetti

third baseman (1981–90),
following the Twins' loss to
Detroit in Game Three of the
1987 ALCS after Minnesota
had grabbed the first two wins
in the series

The first face I saw in the clubhouse [when I got to the big leagues] was Randy Bush. I remember walkin' over to him, going, "Nice to meet you, Mr. Bush," and I shook his hand. Then I saw Kent Hrbek, and I was like, "Wow, how ya doin', Mr. Hrbek?" I called everybody mister. "How ya doin', Mr. Gaetti? How ya doin', Mr. Viola?" It was just respect, that's what it was. That's what you did. I did what rookies should do.

Kirby Puckett
center fielder (1984–95)

⚾ ⚾ ⚾

Some days when I'd come to the ballpark, I'd feel invincible as a player.

Kirby Puckett

Unlike some sports, where many mistakes aren't seen, baseball errors are seen by everyone. Yet you can't brood about them. You have to realize that some day you'll make a play to win a game and you'll be emotionally on top of the world. You have to forget about your errors and look ahead to the next day and the next game. In baseball there's always a tomorrow.

Danny Thompson

⚾ ⚾ ⚾

Baseball is an endurance contest. Who can master the fundamentals? Games are lost, not won, by mental errors.

Rich Rollins

third baseman (1961–68)

⚾ ⚾ ⚾

The Twins were hungry to win. Bert Blyleven kept up good spirit on the team. He relaxed us.

Juan Berenguer

pitcher (1987–90)

What's wrong with y'all today? Did somebody die or somethin'? Hey, there's about twenty-some other teams who'd love to be in the position we're in right now. Even if we lose today, we were here. You should be happy about that. And it's not over yet. We can still win!

Kirby Puckett

to teammates in the quiet Twins clubhouse before the start of Game Six of the 1991 World Series, down three games to two to Atlanta. Puckett would star in the contest, clouting a home run in the bottom of the 11th inning to pull the Series even

Baseball helped me to learn sportsmanship, hard work, desire, and dedication. It helped me to know what it takes to be the best. . . . It was a battle, and I miss it.

Bert Blyleven
pitcher (1970–76, 1985–88)

My calling in life was not to be a superstar ballplayer. I have another job to do: to be a quality player, help my team win, and show kids who have Tourette what they can accomplish.

Jim Eisenreich
outfielder (1982–84)

FAST FACT: Eisenreich was diagnosed with Tourette syndrome in 1982.

If I do it, I do it. If I don't, I don't. I'm never scared to fail.

Kirby Puckett

I feel good about what we in turn gave back to the game of baseball as a group. I only hope that the players today treat the game with the respect and dignity that it deserves.

Tim Laudner

The camaraderie of teammates, learning how to work together . . . baseball taught me a lot of good work ethics. It taught me how to set goals. . . . It can lead to success not only in baseball but in life. Those are lessons you can't buy or read about, you just have to experience them.

Terry Steinbach
catcher (1997–99)

The drive for perfection and the drive for excellence is something that I'll die with.

Terry Steinbach

I'll play, if I have to break a leg to get in there.

Roger Peckinpaugh

*shortstop (1922–26),
prior to Game Six of the 1924
World Series, with the New York
Giants leading three games to two.
Peckinpaugh had missed games
four and five with a severe charley
horse that hemorrhaged in his
thigh. Strapped from ankle to
waist, Peckinpaugh not only took
the field for Game Six but was its
hero. Helping protect a slim 2–1
lead in the ninth, Peckinpaugh
dove to his left and flipped to
second to force the Giants'
potential tying run. The Senators'
shortstop lay motionless on the
ground and had to be carried off
the field, his bound leg muscles
torn, blood soaking his uniform.
Though finished for the rest of the
Series, his effort helped bring
about a Game Seven showdown
that resulted in a Washington win*

Walter Johnson singled to left to open the inning but tried to stretch it into a double. In doing so, he severely strained his leg muscle. He limped off the field and was told to quit by trainer Martin. But Johnson begged to remain in the game and ordered Martin to bandage the muscle. Johnson could scarcely walk but proved himself the best pitcher in baseball on one leg as well as two. In the six innings following his injury, he faced only 20 batters. All told, he yielded six hits in capturing his second game of the 1925 World Series, the third for Washington, which now led Pittsburgh, three to one.

Shirley Povich

Your name stands for what is best in sports and your personal life is held as an example to the youth of our country.

Frank Kellogg

former U.S. secretary of state, during Walter Johnson Day ceremonies on Aug. 2, 1927, celebrating the Big Train's 20th anniversary with the Senators

I never knew Spider-Man could get hurt, but he usually heals fast.

Torii Hunter

after breaking his left ankle climbing the six-foot right-center-field fence at Fenway Park on July 29, an injury that would sideline him the remainder of the 2005 season

I got bone chips in my elbow, my AC joint is separated, I got a broke toe, hamstring, groin—you name it, I got it. It's just the mentality. Some people have to be 100 percent to play; some don't.

Torii Hunter

after the Twins' 9–8 victory over the Arizona Diamondbacks in early June 2005, in which Hunter, playing with a slight shoulder separation, scored the winning run from second base in the ninth after scoring four runs on four hits, including two homers

You can't get too giddy about this game or too down. You have to stay off the roller coaster.

Tom Kelly

That's when you prove how good you are—at the end of the season. You have to finish strong. That's when good players and teams show up.

Johan Santana

pitcher (2000–),
2004 Cy Young Award winner

HUMOR

What did you do, dress in a closet?

Phil Roof

*catcher (1971–76),
to outfielder Danny Walton
(1973, '75), who had shown up
at the airport wearing a red and
white sport coat, blue shirt, white
tie, blue pants, and green shoes*

I don't see past my nose with my left eye when I'm up at that plate. I been hitting .344 as a one-eyed hitter, you know. If I could get two eyes on that ball, I'd hit .600 in this league.

Goose Goslin
*Hall of Fame left fielder
(1921–30, 1933, 1938),
on his pronounced proboscis*

⚾ ⚾ ⚾

My rookie year, I didn't know what to think. It was kind of crazy. I thought he was nuts, laughing and being so loud and talkin' all the time, instigating and stirring up trouble with everybody and then backing his way out.

Chuck Knoblauch
*second baseman (1991–97),
on teammate Kirby Puckett*

This is a deal that's definitely not for the future.

Andy MacPhail

*Twins vice president,
on acquiring 42-year-old
knuckleballer Joe Niekro
from the New York Yankees
in midseason 1987*

Listen, guys, anything can happen in baseball. Washington ain't out of the race yet. Figure it out for yourself. If we win all our 27 games and Detroit loses all their 26 games, we finish in a tie with the Tigers. Now that's worth fighting for, ain't it? And don't forget the team that can't be beat won't be beat. Am I right or am I right?

Al Schacht

*pitcher (1919–21)/coach/later
renowned as the "Clown Prince
of Baseball"*

In my second or third year he said, "You just don't look like you're having much fun. The object is to have some fun: laugh, joke, be you, 'cause what I see now is not you." And he's doing this as he's running off the field and I'm running on the field. He said, "It's just a game. Have some fun."

Ken Griffey Jr.
on Kirby Puckett

Hi, ya, Millie. Been scouting for a husband for you and just brought him in from Kansas City. Meet Joe Cronin.

Joe Engel
Senators scout,
to Clark Griffith's niece and
secretary, Mildred Robertson,
in July 1928. Cronin and
Robertson married six years later

Two thousand bucks!? I can hustle pop bottles and make two thousand bucks!

Kirby Puckett

to a Minnesota Twins scout's initial offer to sign Puckett to a contract

A team broadcaster once gave Junior Ortiz a newspaper article about veteran pitcher and former teammate Rick Reuschel. Mentioned in the story was an anecdote about Reuschel's dislike of visits to the mound, and of a particular instance where he swore at Ortiz. Junior, as the story went, looked back at Reuschel and, addressing him by his nickname, said, "Ooh, Big Daddy, I love when you talk dirty to me."

Tom Kelly

former Twins manager

Ted Robinson

Twins broadcaster and author

Fergie only has a chance if this bus has a flat tire!

Danny Thompson

*to teammates on the Twins' bus
en route from downtown Dallas
to Arlington Stadium, where
Minnesota would open the 1975
season against the Rangers'
Ferguson Jenkins*

Cesar Tovar is the biggest collector in baseball. He takes bats, gloves, balls, batting gloves, anything from anyone. He asks for it in a very nice way, always saying he wants to send it to his three sons in Caracas, Venezuela. He's been in the major leagues for 10 years. He's either running one of the best sporting goods stores in Caracas, or his sons are providing equipment for each team in their Little League.

Danny Thompson

He makes me stop hitting just when I was getting in a groove.

Kirby Puckett

on the bizarre spring training incident of 1987, when Orlando, Fla., police threatened to arrest Puckett if he didn't stop hitting baseballs over Tinker Field's left-field wall. Puckett's power that afternoon shattered a car windshield, reportedly injuring a woman, while two other shots bounced off parked cars

⚾ ⚾ ⚾

Vida Blue put me in the Hall of Fame my rookie year. On Sept. 21, 1970, Blue pitched a no-hitter against the Twins. That box score, with my name in it, is in Cooperstown.

Danny Thompson

⚾ ⚾ ⚾

There's a lot of teasing and needling between blacks and whites. And it's accepted for what it is—humor.

Danny Thompson

On July 12, 1904, Al Orth, a pitcher who was playing center field, made one of the stupidest plays ever pulled by a Washingtonian since John Anderson stole third with the base occupied. Hunter Hill, the St. Louis third baseman, was on second, and pitcher Ralph Glade drove a high fly to center field over Orth's head. Al made a beautiful catch over his shoulder and, to give an additional grandstand effect, kept trotting until he reached the fence. In the meantime, the alert Hill dug out for third, kept on going and scored standing up. Next day Orth was traded to New York.

Morris A. Bealle

FAST FACT: Orth still basks in the glow of the Washington/Minnesota franchise record books, tied for sixth all-time for most losses in a single season (22, in 1903) while ranking third for most complete games in a season (36, in 1902).

Tom Kelly, usually master of the brief cliché, amused scores of writers with stories that bordered on the weird. (He got a call from one man who insisted he should pitch because "the Lord wanted him to." Kelly explained that the Lord's will could not be done because of major-league baseball roster rules.)

Doug Grow

Star Tribune *sportswriter*

I'm starting to think I'm jinxed. Maybe I should change my uniform number from 5 to E–6.

Danny Thompson

on his proclivity to err in the field

Sam Mele: What's he got?
Earl Battey: I don't know, I haven't caught a pitch yet.

> *A pitcher's mound conference between manager Mele, catcher Battey, and young Twins pitcher Dave Boswell, who was facing the Boston Red Sox in one of his early big-league starts. Boswell's first three pitches were clocked for two doubles and a home run*

⚾ ⚾ ⚾

The home run.

Pedro Ramos

when asked to name his best pitch

⚾ ⚾ ⚾

I heard that he was supposed to be a major-league prospect once. If he was a prospect, I was the president of the United States.

Pedro Ramos

on Cuban President Fidel Castro

They had yours professionally erased.

North Dakota sportswriter
to former third baseman Rich Rollins. The writer had once asked Rollins to sign a ball that had also been autographed by Babe Ruth. Rollins expressed concern, checking to be sure if the man wanted Rollins's signature on the valuable ball. Yes, was the man's emphatic reply. Years later, the writer phoned Rollins and informed him that the ball had been auctioned off for charity and that Roger Maris's signature had also been added. The above response came when Rollins asked if his autograph had devalued the ball.

The is home plate, and you stand right here. This is a bat and that guy (Lee Stange) will throw a ball to you. The object is to hit the ball with your bat.

Steve Braun

outfielder (1971–76),
to shortstop Danny Thompson
at batting practice. At that point,
Thompson, benched for a period
of time, had seen little action

It was the 11th homer of my career. I'm only 727 behind Aaron. If I play until I'm 40, I'll only have to average 61 home runs a year to catch him.

Danny Thompson

in a game against the Milwaukee
Brewers and Henry Aaron, who
also hit his 738th round-tripper
that same day, May 17, 1975

Junior Ortiz is so full of garbage, joking constantly, saying one thing and meaning another. I still don't know if the media knew they were getting conned.

Tom Kelly
Ted Robinson

on the Twins' backstop
(1990–91)

⚾ ⚾ ⚾

If I pulled up in front of a restaurant and he came out to park my car, I'd eat somewhere else.

Bob Brenly

catcher/teammate of Juan
Berenguer with San Francisco,
on Berenguer's swarthy
appearance

Pranks and jokes were a big part of Bert Blyleven's notoriety. Cutting off half of someone's tie with scissors, shaving cream in the face, and going to great lengths to execute the perfect hotfoot were all part of his legend. . . . Royals star George Brett and Bert tried to outdo each other in the prank department. During one game when Bert wasn't pitching, he made his way into the Kansas City players' clubhouse, where he cut the toes out of Brett's socks. Brett retaliated by cutting the legs off Blyleven's pants.

Dean Urdahl

LEGENDS

Kirby Puckett is a throwback to the old school, where you do your job the best you can and you accept nothing less than your best performance. It's a lesson a lot of athletes today could learn.

George Brett

Ed Delahanty, one of the greatest batters who ever lived, was induced to jump his contract with the Philadelphia Phillies with a $4,000 offer. . . . When the season was over, it was found that Delahanty was leading the Washington team and the American League with an average of .374.

Morris A. Bealle

*on the great turn-of-the-century
Hall of Famer who played the
last two years of a 16-year major-
league career with the Senators*

When the team returned from a disastrous western trip, 3,500 turned out to welcome Delahanty and cheered every move he made. Management showed a maximum of stupidity in handling him. He was put in right field because triple-chinned Kip Selbach wanted to play left. Delahanty sulked then went on a binge, which proved to be his last one. In Cleveland, he threatened to kill himself. Jimmy Ryan, his roommate, calmed him down and induced him to take the boat ride to Detroit with the team, thinking it might help him sober up. When the team packed up to come back to Washington, Delahanty's uniform was in his room, but he was nowhere to be found. He had completely disappeared.

Morris A. Bealle
on the strange events of July 2, 1903, involving Ed Delahanty

On July 7, manager Loftus received a telegram from the superintendent of the Pullman Company at Buffalo saying a passenger answering Delahanty's description had been put off a train at the International Bridge after an altercation with the conductor and several passengers. Two days later his body was found 11 miles below the bridge and just below the Canadian Niagara Falls. It was completely nude except for the necktie and shoes. One leg was severed. It was believed the body had become entangled in the propeller of the sightseeing boat *Maid of the Mist.*

Morris A. Bealle

A reconstruction of the tragedy revealed that Delahanty had boarded a train at Detroit for New York. In the dining car, he had had six drinks and became loud and boisterous. He began pulling passengers out of their berths and waved a razor at the Pullman porter. The train conductor ejected him at Fort Erie, eight miles west of Buffalo on the Canadian side of the bridge. The bridge tender reported that the ejectee had started across the bridge, which has no footpath, the draw of which was starting to open. Against the bridge tender's protests, Delahanty broke loose. The guard heard a splash in the darkness—and then silence. He didn't even report it to his superiors until questioned a week later.

Morris A. Bealle

At Weiser, Idaho, the semi-pro club of that place had a young gangling six-foot pitcher with arms resembling nothing so much as those of a gorilla. The name was Walter Johnson, and he had the natives of the little Idaho community goggle-eyed with admiration. In Weiser, he had pitched 85 scoreless innings and struck out 166 opposing batsmen in 12 games.

Morris A. Bealle

⚾ ⚾ ⚾

Cliff Blankenship [Washington scout] got a piece of used meat wrapping paper from the hotel cook and wrote out a contract calling for $150 a month, which Walter Johnson signed. Blankenship bought Johnson a one-way ticket to Washington, where he arrived July 20, 1907, with a straw suitcase and a derby hat two sizes too small.

Morris A. Bealle

The Detroit players said they had never faced such blinding speed and, until they started to bunt in the eighth inning, and Johnson's long arms and big feet became tangled in each other trying to field the ball, they were in a fair way to becoming humiliated by a rookie pitcher.

> **Morris A. Bealle**
> on *Walter Johnson's major-league debut, a 3–2 loss to the Tigers on Aug. 2, 1907*

There was a bright hue to the Nationals' rainbow in the development of pitcher Walter Johnson. Johnson gives evidence of being a phenom and they bloom only once in 10 years. His physique and easy swing should keep him in the pitching business for at least 15 years.

> ***Washington Evening Star***
> on *Johnson's big-league debut*

Walter Johnson

MINNESOTA TWINS

On Labor Day weekend 1908, the greatest pitching record ever compiled by a single individual in professional baseball was made by Walter Johnson. . . . On Friday, September 4, Johnson pitched against the New York Yankees, held them to six hits, and shut them out, 3 to 0. On Saturday, Johnson held the Yankees to three hits in a 6–0 win. There was no Sunday baseball in New York at that time. The next game was September 7, Labor Day. The Kansas Cyclone went in the box and again shut out the Yankees on only two hits. The rapturous *Star* bannered this feat with "Wonderful Walter Johnson Again Downs the Yankees; Shuts Them Out For the Third Straight Time."

Morris A. Bealle

To what heights Walter Johnson might have climbed if he had a catcher capable of holding his speed in 1910 dazzles the imagination. Gabby Street, who had been riding to fame as Johnson's batterymate, was injured and out of the game for long periods, and Johnson admitted that he was forced to ease up in pitching to Street's substitutes.

Shirley Povich

The figure of Walter Johnson dominated any comparison. Thirty-eight years old, he still possessed an indefatigable arm and a courageous heart which drove him to greater effort, when his legs and his energy told him to quit.

Shirley Povich

If Walter Johnson was number one in the hearts of Washington fans, Goose Goslin was certainly number two. . . . They forgave his malfeasances in the outfield, admired his contempt for the fences, and the sturdiness of his skull that was being put to almost daily tests by the Goose's crashes against the wall in his brave but futile chases for fly balls.

Shirley Povich

Sept. 16, 1921, was one of those red-letter days that the Washington team occasionally has. It was this day that a powerfully built, shuffling, large-nosed gentleman, who looked more like the famous Honus Wagner, reported for duty. His name was Leon Goslin. He immediately was nicknamed the "Wild Goose of the Potomac" by Denman Thompson, sports editor of the *Washington Star*.

Morris A. Bealle

Goose Goslin

National Baseball Hall of Fame Library, Cooperstown, N.Y.

By 1924, Goslin was solidly established as one of the league's better hitters, a real power hitter. . . . He was still using the same exaggerated closed stance, getting his tremendous power from a swing fuller than any other in the league. His back was nearly turned to the pitcher, and he stood poised for the pitch while looking over his own right shoulder, with his face in profile.

Shirley Povich

on Goose Goslin, entering Washington's world-championship season, his fourth with the team

Goslin was a hitter on the Ruth order.

Bucky Harris

Goslin is a youngster with more width and heft than height. He swings a heavy bat like it was a toothpick in a manner bespeaking confidence. Goslin pulled a heavy vote on the first-impression ballot.

Denman Thompson

Washington Star *sports editor, 1921, on Goose Goslin's debut with the Senators*

🪀 🪀 🪀

I sure do owe a lot to the Babe. But I'll be giving that lad lessons next year.

Goose Goslin

after Game Four of the 1924 World Series, in which Goslin hit a three-run home run, smacked three singles, drove in four runs, and scored twice. Prior to the game, Ruth had journeyed onto the playing field reportedly to give Goslin some hitting advice, which prompted the Goose's tongue-in-cheek reply

A tall young first baseman named Mickey Vernon became Washington's regular first baseman in 1941 and won a pair of American League batting titles (1946, 1953).

Shirley Povich

FAST FACT: Vernon, who suited up as a Senator for 14 years, also led the American League in doubles three times, fielding percentage four times, and was a five-time AL All-Star with Washington.

In 1959 Jim Lemon tied two major-league records by hitting two home runs (one a grand slam) and driving in six runs in one inning. In the 1960 campaign, Lemon battled for the American League home-run championship with Mickey Mantle and Roger Maris. He lost out to Mantle, 40–38.

Dean Urdahl

on the "Covington Clouter,"
a 10-year Washington Senators/
Minnesota Twins outfielder
(1954–63)

Camilo Pascual pitched in several memorable opening days for the Senators. In 1956, which featured an opening-day match up between the Senators and the Yankees, each team hit three home runs. Mickey Mantle rapped two homers—a couple of tape-measure shots off Camilo. In 1960, with President Dwight Eisenhower in attendance, he struck out 15 batters.

Dean Urdahl

I could have caught him with a pair of pliers.

Earl Battey

on the ease of catching Camilo Pascual, who still ranks fourth all-time in franchise wins (145), second in shutouts (31), and third in strikeouts (1,885)

No one worked harder to make himself into a baseball player than Bob Allison. He was a good-looking, rugged guy who set the tone for our ball club. He slid hard, starting about three feet from the base, and would sometimes tear them out of the ground. When teams played the Twins, they knew they were in for a good, clean, tough ballgame, and Bob had a lot to do with that. He was a classy guy on the field and in the community.

Frank Quilici

A former fullback at Kansas University, Bob Allison would crash into linebackers. Once he collided with Chicago catcher Duane Josephson so hard that Josephson's glove flew off and sailed two rows into the stands. His teammates used to call him Mr. America, but to me he was Mr. Indestructible.

Herb Carneal

on the Senators/Twins outfielder from 1958 through '70

Jim Kaat was one of the greatest all-around athletes ever to wear a Twins uniform. For 13 years, he was an ace of the Twins' staff. He pitched 25 years in the big leagues, won 16 consecutive Gold Gloves, had 15 double-digit victory seasons, hit 16 home runs, and often used his exceptional speed as a pinch runner.

Dean Urdahl

The highlight of my Twins career was winning the 1965 American League pennant and going to the World Series for the first time. There were several individual moments that stood out that year. I pitched the pennant clincher against Washington on September 26, and Game Two of the World Series against Sandy Koufax.

Jim Kaat
pitcher (1959–73)

Jim's best year in baseball was 1966. He was 25–13 and led the league with 41 starts, 19 complete games, and 304 innings. *The Sporting News* selected Kaat as American League Pitcher of the Year. But in those years, only one pitcher in all of baseball received the Cy Young Award. It was given to Sandy Koufax.

Dean Urdahl

FAST FACT: Kaat still ranks first or second in 12 total-season and career Twins pitching categories.

Jim Kaat

MINNESOTA TWINS

Jim threw what we call a "heavy" ball, which is a catcher's nightmare. He kept the ball fairly low, and that was back in the days of two-handed catchers. When you catch a low ball, you have to catch it palms up, and it's hard to cushion. Jim's heavy ball with sinking rotation would tear up my hands, but it was hard to hit.

> **Earl Battey**
> *catcher (Wash: 1960;*
> *Minn: 1961–67),*
> *on Jim Kaat*

He may be one of our two eldest players and may be playing on one leg due to five operations on his right knee, but he's one of our best competitors.

> **Danny Thompson**
> *on Tony Oliva*

Tony Oliva

Young Pedro Oliva was recommended by former Senators outfielder Roberto Fernandez to Washington scout Joe Cambria, who signed him to a contract in 1960. Because of hostile political relations between Cuba and the United States, Pedro traveled to America by way of Mexico, using his brother Tony's passport. From that time on, Pedro became Tony Oliva, changing the identity he'd carried since birth on July 20, 1940, in Pinar del Rio, Cuba.

Dean Urdahl

Tony Oliva was critical in teaching me the art of hitting. He deserves to be in the Hall of Fame, and I want to go to Cooperstown for him.

Rod Carew
second baseman/first baseman
(1967–78)

Oliva became the first great DH. Although forced to limp around the bases, he hit .291 with 16 homers and 92 RBIs [in 1973]. Tony slugged the first home run ever recorded by a DH on April 6, 1973, in Oakland.

Dean Urdahl

> *FAST FACT:* Oliva severely injured his right knee on a defensive play in the outfield in 1971 against Oakland. After seven knee operations, and DHing for the next four years, he retired following the 1976 season.

⚾ ⚾ ⚾

Tony Oliva should be in the Hall of Fame. Ask any pitcher in the sixties who the toughest hitter was. They'll tell you it was Tony.

Rich Rollins

⚾ ⚾ ⚾

The man could really, really hit, and he could really, really run.

Frank Kostro
outfielder (1964–65, 1967–69), on Rod Carew

This is your second baseman. End of discussion.

Calvin Griffith

Washington Senators/Minnesota Twins owner (1955–84), to manager Sam Mele about rookie Rod Carew at the start of spring training 1967

Carew tied a major-league record when he stole home seven times in 1969. The Twins won the Western Division championship that year.

Dean Urdahl

Even though he won the batting title in 1969, Rod Carew overshadowed that performance with his exciting baserunning. He had 19 stolen bases, and seven were of home plate, breaking Ty Cobb's American League record and tying Pete Reiser's major-league record.

Herb Carneal

Rod Carew

MINNESOTA TWINS

In 1972, he became the first player ever to win a batting championship without hitting a home run.

Dean Urdahl

on Carew

🏐 🏐 🏐

There's nobody alive who could turn a single into a double, a double into a triple the way Rod could. He may have been the most complete player of his time.

Frank Quilici

🏐 🏐 🏐

I like my uniform clean. If I go out and slide for a ball and the suit gets messy, I go in and I change.

Rod Carew

I want you to go out there and hit .400 so these guys (media) will get off my rear end.

Ted Williams

Boston Red Sox Hall of Famer and the last man to hit .400 or better (.406 in 1941), to Rod Carew, when the Twins' star garnered universal attention by batting over .400 up to the All-Star break in 1977

Carew's offensive exploits with the Twins were impressive. He amassed over 200 hits four times. Three times he led the league in hits, and once he led in runs scored. Rod's 239 hits in 1977 were the highest total in 47 years. The 128 runs he scored in 1977 were the most since 1961.

Dean Urdahl

Bert Blyleven is one of the league's best young pitchers. He celebrated his 24th birthday two days ago, yet he already has won 80 major-league games.

Danny Thompson
1975

Maybe the ball was juiced, maybe my arm was juiced, or I hung too many balls. I knew I had a team behind me that could score runs. Sometimes I'd throw a pitch, and, when it was hit, I'd think it was going to the warning track. When it kept going over the fence, I'd be shocked.

Bert Blyleven

on serving up a major-league-record 50 home runs in 1986, 42 of which were solo shots

Bert Blyleven

MINNESOTA TWINS

Where some pitchers' curves move inches, the break in Blyleven's measured in feet. When at its best, Bert's curve went from shoulder to ankle, a drop from two to seven o'clock.

Dean Urdahl

I had never been so dominated by a pitcher. I couldn't catch up with his fastball, and I couldn't touch his curveball. He struck me out three times. His curveball was among the best I've ever seen.

Mike Kingery
on Bert Blyleven

Both those records say something about our first baseman.

Tom Kelly

on third baseman Gary Gaetti's 45-game and shortstop Greg Gagne's 47-game club-record streaks without an error, during the 1987 season, more than ably assisted by first baseman Kent Hrbek

You aren't going to get much that's loonier than the picture of Kent Hrbek crawling out of bed between Games Six and Seven, grabbing a shotgun, and shagging ducks while four million people begin the sweaty countdown to what all good Nordics call Valhalla.

Jim Klobuchar

1987

MINNESOTA TWINS

Kent Hrbek

A lot of players have spent sleepless nights before Game Seven of a World Series. Kent Hrbek got a call from a duck-hunting buddy who told him the ducks were flying at a favorite spot near Litchfield, 65 miles west of Minneapolis. Kent spent the morning of the biggest game in his life in a duck blind. . . . He admitted that he was too excited and couldn't sleep anyway. "Tom Kelly would kill me if he knew."

Dean Urdahl

on the morning of Oct. 25, 1987

A lot of people say Herbie should have been taken better care of himself, that he might have been a Hall of Famer had he been more serious about the game. I think that's unfair. He did a great job both in the field and at the plate for the Twins. . . . It was a game to him—just like it should be. He was serious about winning, but he was also serious about having a good time and enjoying himself.

Herb Carneal

on Kent Hrbek

You don't find too many players like Kirby Puckett. Those kinds of guys come along every 20, 30 years.

Tony Oliva

*outfielder/designated hitter
(1962–76)*

Kirby Puckett

We've long since learned there's no necessary connection between the qualities that make a great athlete and those that make an admirable person. But Kirby stands out as a refreshing reminder that sometimes the best players can be the best people.

Bob Costas

⚾ ⚾ ⚾

Good defense isn't sexy, unless it's Kirby Puckett dramatically soaring over a wall to pull in a grand slam.

Steve Aschburner

Star Tribune *sportswriter*

⚾ ⚾ ⚾

If you've seen Kirby Puckett, really, he didn't look like a ballplayer. He looked like a roly-poly load, a big fat guy, you know? But, hey, he could hit the ball hard, he had a great arm, he could field and run and do everything.

Tony Oliva

Here was this little guy comes off the bench, and I watched him walk from the dugout to home plate—short, stocky, a big smile on his face. He gets a base hit, makes his turn at first base, and comes back to the bag with this big smile. "How ya doin', Mr. Carew?" I look at him and said, "I'm not Mr. Carew, I'm just Rod." He says, "Oh no, you're Mr. Carew to me right now."

Rod Carew
on Kirby Puckett

Now that you think back on everything about Kirby, the first thing that comes into my mind is that he never said anything. Now it's a complete turnaround, where he don't ever shut up.

Tom Kelly

When you look at one guy that really was the nucleus of that ball club, it was definitely Kirby Puckett. If you're strong up the middle—and there's Kirby standing out in center field as the iron post out there—and you get quality pitching at certain times, we end up winning the World Series. Anytime you could rub that head of Kirby Puckett, there was a lot of luck in there.

Bert Blyleven

If I was pitchin', I'd throw three behind him. Because he can't hit them.

Ken Griffey Jr.
on Kirby Puckett

The *Minneapolis Star Tribune* named Kirby Puckett "Minnesota's Most Important Sports Figure of the Twentieth Century."

Dean Urdahl

⚾ ⚾ ⚾

He's our Michael Jordan, our Larry Bird.

Dave St. Peter

Twins president,
on Kirby Puckett

⚾ ⚾ ⚾

He said I looked like some mechanic guy.

Dan Gladden

on the nickname "Wrench,"
given to him by teammate Kent
Hrbek for Gladden's commonly
dirty uniform, a testament to his
all-out style of play

Frank Viola had a good arm when he first came up in 1982, but he couldn't control his emotions well. He eventually matured and turned the corner with his circle change-up, learned from Johnny Podres, the Twins' pitching coach in the 1980s. Frank would make a circle with his index finger and thumb, grip the ball with the other three fingers, and throw it with the same motion as for his fastball. Depending on how it left his hand, the ball acted like a screwball, breaking down and away from a right-handed batter, and the reduced speed threw off a hitter's timing.

Herb Carneal

Frank Viola

MINNESOTA TWINS

Jack Morris grew up in Highland Park near here, watching Jim Kaat, Mudcat Grant, Bob Allison, and Harmon Killebrew play for the Twins. And he dreamed of doing the same.

Jack Buck

1991 World Series TV broadcaster

⚾ ⚾ ⚾

Jack Morris is without a doubt the gold-standard for World Series guts.

Eric Neel

page Two
ESPN.com

⚾ ⚾ ⚾

Molitor changed how the designated-hitter position could be played. Paul used a high batting average and speed, not just power. His play changed the position.

Dean Urdahl

Torii Hunter

MINNESOTA TWINS

Torii Hunter has a major impact on defense. He tells the left fielder and the right fielder to take the day off and he covers the whole outfield.

Ken Macha

Oakland A's manager

He comes as advertised. He's blowing up at 96 at times, and he's got a 20-mph gap with his change-up. He has a pretty good idea what he's doing, and the last couple of years he's just really gotten a lot of confidence.

Bob Melvin

Arizona Diamondbacks manager, on Johan Santana, following Minnesota's 10–0 victory over the D-backs on June 8, 2005, in which Santana extended his road winning streak to 15–0 in 17 starts, dating back to a loss at Kansas City in May 2004. With the win, Santana (7–2) stretched his major-league strikeout lead to 114

This guy is absolutely the ultimate example of a guy trusting his stuff. . . . He has three pitches he can throw for strikes at any time. He trusts his stuff. And he just pounds the strike zone with it.

Rick Anderson

on Johan Santana

He's always good. Today he was off the charts. That's the best I've seen from him, which is saying something.

Paul Konerko

Chicago White Sox first baseman, on Johan Santana's 5–0 masterpiece over the Sox, Sept. 17, 2005—a four-hit, 13-strikeout gem over eight innings

In my mind, it's Santana, and he's as close to the best as it comes.

Brandon McCarthy

Chicago White Sox pitcher

FAST FACT: Santana pitched tougher against Chicago in 2005 than any other team, at one point hurling $21^1/_3$ scoreless innings against the White Sox. The left-hander was 4–0, had an 0.86 ERA, and allowed just 20 hits in $31^1/_3$ innings in his four previous starts against Chicago before his 4–1 triumph on September 22.

He didn't even look like he was sweating, for God's sake. You've got to at least sweat!

Buddy Bell

*Kansas City Royals manager,
on the performance of Johan
Santana in a 3–1 Twins victory,
Sept. 27, 2005, in which the hurler
struck out six en route to his 15th
victory of the season, extending
his major-league-leading total to
229. Santana's 2.92 ERA tied him
with Cleveland's Kevin Millwood
for first in the American League,
giving him at least a share of the
lead in two of the three major
pitching categories.*

I wanted to show it wasn't a fluke last year. The numbers are there and the stats are there.

Johan Santana

in defense of his credentials for a second straight Cy Young Award in 2005

FAST FACT: Santana went 8–2 after the 2005 All-Star break, logging an impressive 1.88 ERA.

I'm a little biased, but I think he's the best. There's other guys that have better numbers . . . but to me, it doesn't get much better than Johan in this league. Not much better than him. He's the man.

Ron Gardenhire

MINNESOTA TWINS

Johan Santana

Though we gladly salute Bartolo Colon for a terrific year, some of us still aren't so sure the right guy got the trophy. . . . What this voting really proves is that Cy Young voters are still mushy traditionalists who value the almighty "win" above all other indicators of who pitched best over six grueling months. . . . Santana piled up 81 more strikeouts, beat Colon in ERA by 61 points, and had more innings pitched, complete games, and shutouts. . . . Hitters who faced Colon had a batting average of .254 against him. The on-base percentage against Santana was .250. Any more objections, your honor?

Jayson Stark

ESPN.com

FAST FACT: In 2005, Santana finished 16–7 with a 2.87 ERA and a major-league-best 238 strikeouts.

6

SHRINE
TO NO. 3

They called him "the Killer." Harmon Killebrew. In baseball parlance, he was pure power; 573 times he circled the bases with home runs. He played 14 years with the Minnesota Twins. For most of those years, his name was synonymous with baseball in Minnesota.

Dean Urdahl

Griff, that Killebrew kid is even better than Herman [Welker, former Idaho senator] claimed. He has the finest wrist action I've ever seen. He hits them like Mantle. Somebody else will sign him if we don't.

Ossie Bluege

third base (1922–39)/longtime Senators/Twins scout, to owner Clark Griffith, upon scouting Killebrew in an Idaho semi-pro league in the early 1950s after the 17-year-old had just graduated high school

If Harmon Killebrew's home runs could be split into singles, he'd be baseball's only .550 hitter. If they could be laid end to end, they'd stretch from Metropolitan Stadium to Faribault, with enough left over for a side trip to Northfield.

Arno Goethal

former St. Paul Dispatch *executive sports editor*

He hit 559 home runs in his years with the Griffith organization and ranked fifth on the all-time list behind Hank Aaron, Babe Ruth, Willie Mays, and Frank Robinson. He was the last original Twin, too, coming to Minnesota in 1961 when Calvin Griffith moved the franchise from Washington, D.C.

Danny Thompson
on franchise legend
Harmon Killebrew

In 1960, he became the first player in 25 years to hit a homer onto the left-field roof at Tiger Stadium in Detroit. Two years later, Harmon topped that by rocketing one completely over the Detroit left-field roof. He came just short of putting one out of Memorial Stadium in Baltimore.

Dean Urdahl

The man who can swing the bat the fastest is the man who'll hit the most home runs.

Harmon Killebrew

Harmon's most monumental home run came at Metropolitan Stadium on June 3, 1967, against the Angels off Lew Burdette. He rifled a shot six rows into the upper deck in left field, shattering two seats, 520 feet from home plate. The spot is now commemorated with a red chair mounted high on a wall in the Mall of America, which was built at the former Metropolitan Stadium site. Home plate's location is commemorated as well by a metal plaque in a main-level floor at the mall.

Dean Urdahl

I got the book on how to pitch to Harmon Killebrew from my roommate.

Jack Sanford

*California Angels pitcher,
after serving up a tape-measure
shot to Killebrew, on June 4,
1967, that hit the facing of the
upper deck at Metropolitan
Stadium. The previous day,
Killebrew hit the longest home
run in the Met's history off
Sanford's roommate, Lew
Burdette—a moon shot that
landed in the second row of
upper deck seats in left field*

Killebrew was the first to clear everything, double deck and the roof, in Detroit's left field. Since then Willie Horton of the Tigers has been the only other batter to reach the street in that direction.

Dick Cullum

late Minneapolis Tribune *writer*

In my opinion, the hardest ball I ever hit was in Chicago, off Herb Score. I hit it about three-quarters of the way up one of the posts in the upper deck in left field. I hit it so hard the ball bounced all the way back to shortstop.

Harmon Killebrew

FAST FACT: Killebrew's launch off Score took place on Aug. 6, 1960.

◯ ◯ ◯

Harmon Killebrew epitomized raw power.

National Baseball Hall of Fame

◯ ◯ ◯

One time I hit a grand-slam home run for Washington and they sent me down to Charlotte the next day.

Harmon Killebrew

A scribe once criticized The Whammer for not showing enough emotion. "The guy is no team leader. He doesn't crackle. His quotes aren't that hot." I only thought to myself, "Maybe not. But when he hitches up the pants and trots the lumber to the plate, everybody in the park can feel the tension and the threat. He's a leader all right."

Don Riley

former St. Paul Pioneer Press *writer*

Killebrew gives us class. He makes us feel like we are all riding in a Cadillac.

Earl Battey

Harmon Killebrew

MINNESOTA TWINS

Harmon was a better fielder than people think. He wasn't fast, but he was quick. His initial moves were good. His hands were quick. I had him for some games in the outfield, but he was better in the infield.

Sam Mele

*outfielder (Wash: 1949–52)/
manager (Minn: 1961–67)*

Eight times Killebrew hit over 40 home runs in a season. During 10 seasons, he cracked over 30 homers, and nines time he drove in over 100 runs. Harmon was named the American League's MVP in 1969 when he hit 49 home runs, drove in 140 runs, and walked 145 times to lead the league in all three categories.

Dean Urdahl

The guy who gave me more trouble than anybody else was a little relief pitcher, Stu Miller. . . . I think I got two hits off him in five years. Miller was slow, but his motion was so deceptive. He was the first pitcher I ever saw who took a stretch with nobody on base.

Harmon Killebrew

As of 2006, Killebrew still held team records for home runs, runs-batted-in, and walks. Harmon's jersey number 3 was retired by the Twins in a ceremony on Aug. 11, 1974. He became the first Twin elected to the Baseball Hall of Fame, on Jan. 10, 1984.

Dean Urdahl

FAST FACT: Killebrew is also the franchise leader, including the team's 60 years in Washington, in games played (2,329), total bases (4,026), and strike-outs (1,629).

Every day when I walked on the field is my favorite memory.

Harmon Killebrew

Killebrew was a fierce competitor, a solid fielder, and most important, the Twins' quiet leader year after year.

Dave Mona
Dave Jarzyna

Harmon's Twins uniform, number 3, is the first ever retired by the Griffith organization.

Danny Thompson

After the 1974 season, Killebrew signed with the Kansas City Royals. On May 4, 1975, he returned to Metropolitan Stadium for the first time. His Twins uniform No. 3 was retired in a pre-game ceremony, and in his first at-bat, he homered to left. The fans cheered as Killebrew rounded the bases in what was probably the loudest ovation ever have given a member of the opposition.

Dave Mona
Dave Jarzyna

It was a dramatic moment because only minutes earlier he had stood at home plate while Calvin Griffith announced that number 3 would never be worn by another Minnesota player.

Danny Thompson
on Killebrew's nostalgic homer, then as a member of the Kansas City Royals, against his former team, May 4, 1975

I remember my 500th career home run. Hit that at the Met off Mike Cuellar in the first inning, in 1971. It had been a long time between 499 and 500, and when I got back to the bench Bill Rigney [Twins manager] said he hoped it wasn't that long between 500 and 501. I got number 501 the same night.

Harmon Killebrew

Harmon Killebrew told me never to chew gum at the plate. He said it makes your eyeballs bounce up and down.

Charlie Manuel

former Cleveland Indians coach

He hit line drives that put the opposition in jeopardy. And I don't mean infielders, I mean outfielders.

Ossie Bluege

My father used to play with my brother and me in the yard. Mother would come out and say, "You're tearing up the grass." "We're not raising grass," Dad would reply. "We're raising boys."

Harmon Killebrew

Harmon Killebrew was one of the people who I didn't include in the *Baseball* documentary. Not because I didn't respect him or didn't think he was important, but because you can't be an encyclopedia and tell a good story.

Ken Burns

documentarian

Teenage Harmon Killebrew signed with the Washington Senators and aged as a Minnesota Twin. . . . He threatened pitchers enough to draw more than 100 walks a season a total of seven times.

Gerald Astor

writer/author

If ever anyone wielded a blunt instrument at home plate, it was Harmon Killebrew. There was nothing subtle about the Idaho strongboy, and it was always his intention to mash a pitched ball as hard and as far as he could.

Donald Honig
author/historian

Killebrew can knock the ball out of any park, including Yellowstone.

Paul Richards
former Baltimore Orioles manager

I'll always think of him as a good friend. As a rookie, it's difficult to realize what's going on, or where you're at. But when I joined the club in 1970, Harmon helped me through that difficult time by accepting me right away. It wasn't until my leukemia was discovered, however, that I realized what a true friend he was.

Danny Thompson

⚾ ⚾ ⚾

The team without Harmon Killebrew is like dressing up for a formal affair with white tie and tails and then wearing muddy shoes.

Earl Battey

⚾ ⚾ ⚾

I didn't have evil intentions, but I guess I did have power.

Harmon Killebrew

FIELD BOSSES

Let's insult 'em first, and then beat their brains out.

Bucky Harris

his call to arms to his players before a late-September series against the White Sox, who had made it known they would prefer the Yankees to win the 1924 American League pennant, not the Senators

A Special Delivery letter arrived. The envelope had the Washington Club stamp on it. I had to blink my eyes, as I read the message in Clark Griffith's own handwriting. My hand shook. I had to sit down. I knew then how a man feels when he gets word that an unknown relative has left him a fortune. The letter offered me the job as manager of the Washington Club.

Bucky Harris

*hired in 1924 as the Senators'
player-manager at age 27, the
youngest manager to that time
in major-league history*

You're on your way up, Bucky. Griffith likes you. He liked those hits you made and the way you stuck in there with that finger.

George Wiltse

manager, minor-league team in Buffalo, New York, to second baseman Bucky Harris, who had drawn the attention of Senators owner Clark Griffith with his gutsy, all-out play. On the day Griffith scouted Harris, the infielder went 6-for-8 in a twin bill—playing both games with a finger broken in three places. Harris would go on to become one of the great managers in Senators/Twins history

Bucky Harris

MINNESOTA TWINS

I didn't know I was going to be the manager of this club a month ago. Far be it from me to tell you fellows how to play ball—but what I'm asking is that you go out there and make me a good manager.

Bucky Harris

to his players at the beginning of spring training 1924, on his promotion to player-manager of the Senators at the age of 27

Joe Cronin's a scrapper. He thinks nothing but baseball. I like these young fellows who fight for everything. I made no mistake with Bucky Harris. I think I have another Harris.

Clark Griffith

Cronin, like Harris, would become a player-manager for Griffith, finishing second in American League MVP balloting in 1933, the same year he was named manager of the Senators and guided them to the AL pennant. At 26, he became the youngest man ever to manage in the major leagues

There were two ways to manage: through fear, like Billy Martin, or be like Sam Mele and just let players play.

Harmon Killebrew

Being fair and still being firm.

Sam Mele

on good managing

Some people thought Billy Martin was after my job. That wasn't true. Whenever he helped us to win, it helped me keep my job that much longer.

Sam Mele

If running were so important, Jesse Owens could have won 30 games.

Johnny Sain

*pitching coach (1965–66),
on his philosophy that running,
and therefore the legs, were
secondary to a pitcher's arm
and brain. Pitchers loved Sain's
approach because he didn't
make them run between starts*

Cal Ermer was a solid baseball man and an easygoing guy, usually. He could become riled by losing or by an umpire's call. He was a former soccer player and when he lost an argument with an umpire, he'd tear off his hat, throw it on the ground, and kick it soccer-style.

Herb Carneal

on the Twins' manager from 1967 through '68

Billy Martin is the type of manager who inspires everyone—his players and the opposition's. He'll do anything, or say anything, to beat you.

Danny Thompson

Billy Martin was the best manager I played for. No one wanted to win more than Billy.

Dave Boswell

As far as baseball knowledge, the tops was Billy Martin. He was like a gambler. His instincts for baseball were absolutely phenomenal.

Dean Chance
pitcher (1967–69)

Nowadays, you don't hear much about bench-jockeying, but it's still an important part of baseball. And Martin easily ranks as the league's top agitator.

Danny Thompson

I fondly remember my relationship with Billy Martin, who turned me from a boy to a man.

Rod Carew

Billy worked with me on playing second base, we talked baseball. When I was trying to hit home runs, Billy advised me to use the whole field and not try to hit the ball out of the park.

Rod Carew

⚾ ⚾ ⚾

He had a Napoleon attitude. It was Billy's way or no way.

Rich Reese

on Billy Martin

⚾ ⚾ ⚾

Controversy followed Billy. He had a fistfight with his pitcher, Dave Boswell; publicly debated player moves; and started a pitcher, Bob Miller, in the playoffs against owner Calvin Griffith's wishes. Griffith fired Martin after the season. Billy was extremely popular with Minnesota fans, and his dismissal was a public relations disaster for the Twins.

Dean Urdahl

Billy Martin always seemed most successful in his first year with each team. One of the things that worked against continued success for him was his habit of getting into feuds with his own ballplayers. Some say that he did better in his first year with a team because he overworked the pitching staff. Billy often left the starters in, even after they were tiring in the late innings. He got some good performances out of these pitchers for a couple of years, but they all ended up with bad arms. By that time, of course, Martin was elsewhere.

Herb Carneal

I can't tell you exactly what I'm going to do, but I can tell you one thing, that it won't be anything rational.

Calvin Griffith

on naming Billy Martin's replacement as Twins manager for the 1970 season

Managing sucked. In managing, you're not in control of your own destiny. Calvin [Griffith] and I disagreed on players. We were always fighting on that stuff. I think Calvin thought I was too young to get involved in the player selection and, as a result, we often had a difference of opinion.

Frank Quilici

Things can't go the way they've been going, or we'll have another manager here.

Tom Kelly

during his first spring training, 1987

I've talked to other coaches in football and hockey, and there seems to be a consensus: If players are enjoying what they're doing, the end result seems to be in the right column.

Tom Kelly

⚾ ⚾ ⚾

We don't try to make spectacular plays. We just try to make all the plays we're supposed to make.

Tom Kelly

⚾ ⚾ ⚾

You have to look at players occasionally and evaluate what they can do for your organization down the line.

Tom Kelly

⚾ ⚾ ⚾

Tom Kelly made you more relaxed. If you got hit hard one day, he'd say, "Be ready, I might need you tomorrow." You felt like you got more chances with him.

Juan Berenguer

Tom Kelly was a great leader. Leadership can't be taught.

Randy Bush

outfielder (1982–93)

I agree with the theory that just getting to the World Series is the big thing. Getting through the playoffs is the hard thing. That's the most pressure. The World Series is ice cream on the cake. Once you realize you're there, it takes a lot of pressure off.

Tom Kelly

The longer we're out there in the field, the more chance we have of making mistakes. So we're always talking about, "Get the boys off the field," because everyone knows that when you're hitting, you can't give up any runs.

Ron Gardenhire

MAJOR MOMENTS

The ball went into the left-field bleachers on a line. It was the most important hit of the franchise. I can still see it, the ball going out and the reaction of the crowd. The Yankees never did recover, and we went on to win the pennant.

Bob Casey

longtime Twins public address announcer,
on Harmon Killebrew's two-run homer in the bottom of the ninth with two out and Minnesota trailing, 5–4, in early July 1965

Walter Johnson made his second appearance as a member of the Washington team against Cleveland yesterday and by his performance strengthens the belief he is one of the pitching finds of the season. The hard-hitting Naps were merely pygmies before his vicious speed. His delivery was puzzling. He had terrific speed and a shoot on the ball which baffled the batsmen.

Morris A. Bealle

on Johnson's four-hit, 7–2 win over Cleveland in early August 1907

There was the day he fanned four men in the same inning, yet was scored on.

Shirley Povich

FAST FACT: In beating the Red Sox in his season debut, April 15, 1911, Walter Johnson contributed another chapter to pitching lore. With one batter already gone on strikes, Johnson fanned Larry Gardner, but the ball got away from Senators catcher Eddie Ainsmith. Gardner then stole second, as Johnson put down Harry Hooper for the second out, his third strikeout of the inning. Tris Speaker followed with a double, scoring Gardner, before Johnson struck out the fourth hitter that inning, Duffy Lewis, for the final out.

On Sept. 29, 1924, the Nationals clinched their first pennant in modern baseball times. The Yanks no longer had a mathematical possibility of beating them. The season ended September 30 with the second-place Yankees two and a half games in the rear.

Morris A. Bealle

It was the modest, beloved Walter Johnson and his pitching feats that set new records in the books, who stood virtually alone against the national scorn for Washington's hapless teams of the early 1900s. The reverence toward Johnson displayed by Washington fans spilled over into the national community, and in 1924 America rose in applause for the man who, after toiling uncomplainingly for 17 years on Washington teams, found himself pitching in a World Series.

Shirley Povich

The first and last games of the 1924 World Series went 12 innings and also ended with the score 4 to 3.

Morris A. Bealle

A sharp grounder went toward Freddie Lindstrom at third base, a routine play, and then came a funny bounce! A high, hopping bounce that went over Lindstrom's head into left field for a freak single. The ball hit a pebble perhaps. It scored Muddy Ruel from second base and won the 1924 World Series for the Senators.

Shirley Povich

on the bizarre game-ending and Series-ending play in the bottom of the 12th inning of Game Seven of the '24 World Series that gave Washington a 4–3 victory over the New York Giants and its one and only world-championship crown

Unlike the 1924 Series, the '25 games were played under the most miserable of weather conditions. Some neutral writers blamed Washington's loss on the fact that Walter Johnson pitched the last game from such a mound of muck that he couldn't hold his feet. They criticized the umpire-in-chief for allowing the seventh game to be even started, much less continued, under such impossible playing conditions. The outfielders were said to be invisible from the stands during the last game, with rain pouring steadily, the field thick with mortar-like mud.

Morris A. Bealle

on the Senators' seven-game
World Series loss to Pittsburgh
in 1925

In Yankee Stadium, on April 29, 1933, occurred the unforgettable play of the season . . . a double play at home plate on the same batted ball!

Shirley Povich

FAST FACT: Trailing 6 to 3 in the bottom of the ninth, Yankees Lou Gehrig and Dixie Walker hit singles with no outs, putting runners on first and second. Tony Lazzeri drove a tremendous line smash between Goose Goslin in right field and Fred Schulte in center. Gehrig played it cautiously, hugging second until the ball dropped. Walker, dashing into second, almost ran up Gehrig's back as they lit for home. Goslin made a quick retrieval in deep right-center, and with one of the most powerful throwing arms in the league, whipped it on the fly to Cronin, who had raced far out for the relay. Now it was in the hands of the best relay man in the league. Cronin cut loose a meteor throw to Sewell at the plate, who tagged Gehrig sliding in. Sewell, pirouetting from the force of the tag, then dove back across the plate, ball in hand, to also tag Walker.

For the record baseball price of a quarter of a million dollars, Clark Griffith sold to the Red Sox Joe Cronin, his wonder-boy manager and nephew by marriage.

Shirley Povich

FAST FACT: The astounding sale of nephew-in-law Cronin was not Griffith's idea. Boston owner Tom Yawkey, the deal's catalyst, waved the preposterous sum several times in front of Griffith during the 1933–34 off-season. The more Griffith thought about it, the unusual family angle presented a potential problem should the team falter, and thus the door opened for the blockbuster sale.

Harmon Killebrew was part of an awesome display of power when he became the fourth consecutive Twin to hit a home run in the same inning. The outburst came in the 11th stanza of a game played May 2, 1964, against the Los Angeles Angels; it tied a major-league record.

Dean Urdahl

In the press box a strange drama was unfolding. Charlie Finley, the Kansas City A's owner, had phoned Jim Schaaf, the A's public relations director, to find out how the Twins-A's game was coming. Finley called just as Tony Oliva was stepping into the batter's box in the 10th. Schaaf reported Oliva's home run as it happened. Finley's mood worsened as Jimmie Hall's home run was described. Schaaf then told him Bob Allison had hit one out. Schaaf assured his boss he was telling the truth as the A's changed pitchers. But Harmon Killebrew's home run was too much for Finley. He was so convinced that Schaaf was pulling his leg that he fired him over the phone.

Herb Carneal

on the astonishing Twins barrage against the A's in May 1964 that tied the major-league record of four consecutive home runs

What I remember was the silent reaction of the Yankees. I was sitting on their bench. It was such a dramatic moment, and I had to sit there and hide my emotions.

> **Jim Wiesner**
>
> *visiting clubhouse attendant,*
> *on Harmon Killebrew's two-run*
> *homer that shattered the Yankees*
> *just before the All-Star break in*
> *1965*

⚾ ⚾ ⚾

It was a great Series. I watch that Game Seven on Classic Sports. I must have seen it 10 times, and we lose very time. But it was a thrill.

> **Sam Mele**
>
> *on the 1965 World Series, which*
> *Minnesota lost to the Los Angeles*
> *Dodgers, four games to three*

Killebrew and four teammates slammed five home runs in one inning, carving a record against Kansas City in the seventh frame on June 9, 1966. Rich Rollins, Zoilo Versalles, Tony Oliva, Don Mincher, and Killebrew were the first in American League history to achieve this.

Dean Urdahl

It hit right in the pocket. I felt for the wall when I was going back and knew where I was. I just wanted to make sure that I was squeezing it tightly enough.

Kirby Puckett

on his 1987 opening-night grab of Mickey Tettleton's deep fly beyond the 408-foot marker in center field in the 10th inning, robbing the Detroit catcher of a home run. Minnesota won, 5–4

I've never seen Puckett do that before. It was unbelievable. . . . When a guy makes a catch like that, it seems like your shoulders lift up about eight inches.

George Frazier

pitcher (1986–87),
on Kirby Puckett's game-saving
catch over the center-field wall
in the 1987 season opener
against Detroit

Aug. 3, 1987. The stuff of legends and perhaps the most memorable night of the season. Joe Niekro is busted by the umpires after an emery board and a piece of sandpaper are found in his possession. He is ejected by ump Tim Tschida in the fourth inning at California for scuffing baseballs. Despite the commotion, the Twins rally for an 11–3 victory.

Jerry Zgoda

Star Tribune *compiler*

Fast Fact: Niekro would serve a 10-day suspension for the infractions.

Aug. 14, 1987. Niekro appears on *Late Night with David Letterman* wearing a workman's belt that contains a power sander, nail file, clothes brush, toenail and fingernail clippers, sandpaper, tweezers, scissors, Vaseline, emery boards, and two bottles of Kiwi Scuff Magic.

Jerry Zgoda

Aug. 30, 1987. Kirby Puckett goes 6-for-6, with two doubles, two homers, and four RBI in a 10–6 roller-coaster triumph in Milwaukee. Puckett sets club marks for most hits in consecutive games, hits in one game, and total bases (14). With his 4-for-5 performance Saturday (Aug. 29), Puckett breaks an AL record and ties a major-league mark for most hits in consecutive nine-inning games.

Jerry Zgoda

Kirby Puckett played the greatest 48 hours of baseball of his life. Those two games in Milwaukee produced 10 hits in 11 at-bats, four of them home runs. No one who saw it is ever likely to forget it.

Bob Costas

on the aforementioned play of Puckett, Aug. 29–30, 1987

C'mon, it don't happen to normal people.

Tom Kelly

reflecting on Kirby Puckett's amazing 10-for-11 performance of Aug. 29–30, 1987

That was the biggest play of my major-league career.

Al Newman

second baseman (1987–91), whose first-inning heads-up play in throwing home on the second leg of a double-play ball doubled speedy Kansas City runner Willie Wilson racing in from third. Minnesota went on to an 8–1 triumph over the Royals, which reduced the Twins' magic number to one for clinching the 1987 AL West crown

It's incredible, the best thing that's happened in my baseball career. It's a dream. I can't believe it's happening. It's a fantasy come true.

Steve Lombardozzi

second baseman 1985–88), on clinching the division championship in 1987

I knew we were going to do it. I knew it.

Jim Wiesner

*Twins clubhouse man,
on his gut decision to place the
champagne on ice in the visiting
Twins' locker room at Arlington
Stadium during the third inning
of Minnesota's AL West-clinching
win over the Texas Rangers in
'87. At the time, the Twins were
down, 3–0*

I wanted to make the 1987 highlight film.
Now I'm in Twins history forever.

Steve Lombardozzi

*whose four RBIs on a three-run
homer and run-scoring single
during the Twins' 5–3 win over
Texas on September 28 gave
Minnesota its first division title
in 17 years*

I just want to stand here and feel it. I just want to feel what this is like. I've waited a long time.

Randy Bush

in the afterglow of Minnesota's first division crown in 17 years

This is the year to put up or shut up.

Frank Viola

pitcher (1982–89), before the 1987 world-championship season

I guess we put up.

Frank Viola

following the AL West division-clinching victory over Texas at the close of the '87 season

An ice-cream vendor disappeared in an ocean of white handkerchiefs when Don Baylor creamed a Willie Hernandez pitch in the eighth inning to give the Twins an irrevocable lead over the Detroit Tigers. A bar owner from St. James nearly suffocated an accountant from New Brighton in a bear hug. A weeping grandmother from Plymouth danced something that looked like the boogaloo. It was jubilation, friend. It was a Polish wedding, a Swedish smorgasbord, a piece of Woodstock.

Jim Klobuchar

on reaction to Minnesota's 8–5 Game One triumph over Detroit in the 1987 ALCS

I think some people are starting to believe in us.

Kent Hrbek

following the Twins' Game Two win over Detroit in the 1987 American League Championship Series to take a 2–0 series lead

I thought it was the turning point of the game.

Sparky Anderson

former Detroit Tigers manager, on Tiger first baseman Darrell Evans' being picked off third base in the bottom of the sixth inning of Game Four of the 1987 ALCS to quell a potential Detroit rally. Minnesota held on for a 5–3 victory, their third of the series

Pour.

Gary Gaetti

*his instructions to champagne-
bearing teammate Tom
Brunansky, after Minnesota had
secured the American League
pennant following their 9–5 win
over Detroit to take the 1987
ALCS, four games to one*

It is everybody's dream from the time they are 5 years old. You're in the back yard, and you're pretending you're in the World Series.

Randy Bush

*following the Twins' capture
of the 1987 American League
pennant*

I tried to hold my emotions in a little bit. Thought about putting my flap down like Jeffrey Leonard, but thought twice about that.

Dan Gladden

on his grand-slam home run that broke open Game One of the 1987 World Series, a 10–1 Twins victory over St. Louis

FAST FACT: In the 1987 NLCS, Leonard, a San Francisco Giant, became only the third player in postseason history to win the MVP award while his team lost the series. Leonard hit home runs in each of the first four games, taunting the Cardinals with his slow, deliberate "one-flap-down" trot, with one arm held against his side and the other arm extended.

Minnesota became only the second team ever to hit two grand slams in a World Series. The 1956 Yankees had done it, and so now had the Twins.

Al Michaels

broadcaster,
after Kent Hrbek's grand slam
in Game Six of the 1987 World
Series gave Minnesota a 10–5
win to tie the Series against
St. Louis at three games apiece.
Earlier, in the Twins' Game One
victory, Dan Gladden had
connected with the bases full

They hit all the bad pitches I made, and they hit all the good pitches I made. It was just a bad day all around.

John Tudor

St. Louis Cardinals pitcher,
on his Game Six 10–5 defeat
of Minnesota in the 1987
World Series

You can wave your Homer Hanky until the roof becomes retractable, and it won't happen this way again. A team wins for the first time only once.

Jay Weiner

Star Tribune *sportswriter,*
on the 1987 world-champion
Twins' conquest of St. Louis

⚾ ⚾ ⚾

Can we bottle this all and uncork it again in April?

Jay Weiner

following the Twins' Game Seven
1987 World Series win over
St. Louis

⚾ ⚾ ⚾

I wasn't trying to be a hero or anything, just hit the ball between first and second. I just reacted to the pitch and ended up hitting it out of the park.

Greg Gagne

shortstop (1983–92),
on his Game One three-run
home run in the 1991 World
Series against Atlanta

We forgot about Chili Davis.

Bobby Cox

*Atlanta Braves manager,
on Davis's Game Two two-run
homer off Tom Glavine in the
1991 World Series that put the
Twins up 2–0. The Braves
thought they had staved off a
Minnesota rally by getting Kirby
Puckett, the batter preceding
Davis, to hit into a double play*

People just went berserk. They knew it was gone. I knew I'd hit the ball well, and I think Glavine knew I hit it well. It was so loud in there. I never experienced anything like that, and the curtain call was something I never experienced before. It was exceptional. I felt chills going through me.

Chili Davis

designated hitter (1991–92), on his 1991 World Series Game Two second-inning two-run smash that pushed the Twins to a 2–0 lead

It was a close play. He was safe when he got back to the base. Had he slid, he would have been safe. Problem was he didn't slide, he came back into first base and ran into me and was falling over. I kept the tag on him and his momentum carried him off the bag, and I ended up with his leg in my arm. Everybody was talking like how I tried to pull him off the bag, but he was coming off the bag anyway, and so I just more or less caught him.

Kent Hrbek

*first baseman (1981–94),
on the controversial play at first
base in Game Two of the 1991
World Series. Atlanta's Ron Gant
had singled to left but took a wide
turn off first before beating the
throw back to the bag. Initially, it
looked like Gant had been lifted
off the bag by Hrbek, but umpire
Drew Coble maintained that Gant's
momentum had pulled him off*

Hᴇʏ Hʀʙᴇᴋ, ᴛʜɪs ɪsɴ'ᴛ ᴡʀᴇsᴛʟɪɴɢ, ɪᴛ's ʙᴀsᴇʙᴀʟʟ.

Sign in Atlanta-Fulton County Stadium

greeting Twins first baseman Kent Hrbek upon arrival for Game Three of the 1991 World Series

All right, guys, you gotta jump on my back tonight! I'm gonna carry us tonight." And when I said that, there was a whole different atmosphere in this clubhouse. Everybody started chirping. I guess it was a sigh of relief for them, like, "Whew! I'm glad I'm not going to have to do it," or whatever. But I felt that day I was going to make a difference.

Kirby Puckett

prior to Game Six of the 1991 World Series

Game Six was Kirby Puckett Day.

Chili Davis

on the 1991 World Series, with the Twins returning to the Metrodome down, three games to two, to Atlanta

⚾ ⚾ ⚾

Brilliant play by Kirby Puckett. Look at him time the jump!

Tim McCarver

broadcast analyst, on the Twins center fielder's leaping catch high against the left-center-field wall of the Metrodome to rob Atlanta Braves hitter Ron Gant of an extra-base hit in the third inning of Game Six of the 1991 World Series, with Minnesota leading, 2–0

It was both a beautiful dream and a tension-filled nightmare all wrapped up in one.

Ernie Harwell

legendary play-by-play broadcaster, on the 3–3 deadlock going into the bottom of the seventh inning of Game Six of the 1991 World Series, with Atlanta holding a three-games-to-two edge over Minnesota

Chill, what d'ya think? I'm gonna bunt off this guy.

Kirby Puckett

to on-deck batter Chili Davis, discussing the Atlanta Braves' strategy of bringing in reliever Charlie Leibrandt, a renowned change-up thrower, to face Puckett in the bottom of the 11th inning of Game Six of the '91 World Series

Puck, do you think the people here want to see Chili Davis win this ballgame, or do you think they want to see Kirby Puckett win this ballgame? This is your team, man.

Chili Davis

to Kirby Puckett immediately prior to Puckett's 11th-inning at-bat against the Braves

⚾ ⚾ ⚾

Into deep left-center! . . . And we'll see you tomorrow night!

Jack Buck

his play-by-play call of Kirby Puckett's Game Six-winning home run in the bottom of the 11th inning that left the 1991 World Series tied at three games apiece

⚾ ⚾ ⚾

Puckett single-handedly won the game.

Tom Kelly

on the conclusion of Game Six of the '91 World Series

Somebody's got a storybook, see. Chapter Six is over, and now you turn to Chapter Seven. It's a storybook World Series. What's gonna happen tomorrow in Game Seven—Chapter Seven—oh my God, I can't wait! It's gonna be something. Can you imagine this going on like this? Unbelievable.

Tom Kelly

after the histrionics of Game Six of the 1991 World Series, won by Minnesota on Kirby Puckett's 11th-inning home run

It's all pitching here tonight. Jack Morris, John Smoltz, nine hits total—the longest scoreless start of a seventh game in a World Series.

Jack Buck

1991

And so the stage was set for the incredible eighth inning of the seventh game, perhaps the most nail-biting complete inning in the history of the World Series.

Ernie Harwell

*after seven scoreless innings
in Game Seven of the 1991
World Series*

FAST FACT: With one out in the top of the eighth, the Braves put runners on first and third, before pinch hitter Sid Bream hit into an inning-ending double play. In the Twins' bottom half, pinch hitter Randy Bush opened with a single. After a popup for the first out, Chuck Knoblauch singled. Runners on first and third. Mike Stanton relieved starter John Smoltz and walked Kirby Puckett intentionally. Just as the Braves hit into an inning-ending double play in the top half, Kent Hrbek then lined to second, doubling the runner, Knoblauch, off second base.

It was the biggest play of the Series by far.

Ernie Harwell

on the double-play ball off the bat of Atlanta's Sid Bream— first to home plate to first—in the top of the eighth inning of the seventh game of the 1991 World Series, preserving a scoreless tie to that point

⚾ ⚾ ⚾

Larkin is the pinch hitter, with the bases loaded and one out . . . the Minnesota bench hoping to get this winning run across here in the 10th that's carried by Dan Gladden at third. . . . Pena in a jam. . . . The Twins are gonna win the World Series! The Twins have won it! It's a base hit! It's a 1–0 10-inning victory!

Jack Buck

his play-by-play call on the final play of the 1991 World Series

Nineteen ninety-one was very special, because of that one hit in Game Seven. Every October people bring that hit up, so some way it'll always be remembered. . . . It was a perfect situation. I was a contact hitter, and you just want to put the ball in play. The outfield and infield were playing in. Outside of the situation being very nerve-wracking, it was a situation that a lot of hitters should succeed in.

Gene Larkin

on his bases-loaded, game- and World Series-winning hit to left field in the bottom of the 10th inning to clinch the 1991 world championship for Minnesota

I made a pretty good pitch in a critical situation against a hitter I respected tremendously.

Jack Morris

pitcher (1991),
on his performance in the sixth
inning of a scoreless Game Seven
of the 1991 World Series. With
Atlanta runners on first and third,
two out, and a 3–2 count on the
Braves' Ron Gant, Morris iced
him with an outside-corner
fastball to close out the side

After the ninth inning, Kelly said, "You did a good job. That's enough." I said, "No, it isn't. It's my game."

Jack Morris

on manager Tom Kelly's attempt to relieve Morris in the critical Game Seven of the 1991 World Series. Morris would pitch another scoreless inning in the 10th before Gene Larkin's game-winning hit in the bottom of the inning gave the Twins their second world championship in five years

I was excited about coming home and playing in front of my family and friends. I was also excited about being teammates with my man, Kirby. But the 3,000th hit, at home, was by far the highlight of my Twins career.

Dave Winfield

outfielder (1993–94)

He could have outlasted Methuselah.

Anonymous Twin Cities sportswriter

on Jack Morris's Game Seven masterpiece in the 1991 World Series

Less than a month into the 1994 season, on a Wednesday night game against the Milwaukee Brewers at the Metrodome, Scott Erickson pitched the Twins' first no-hitter in 27 years. Scott had been up and down ever since his 20-win season in 1991 but really had his stuff that night. When Erickson's pitching well, he keeps the ball low and the batters hit a lot of ground balls. On this night he struck out five, got seven batters on fly balls or line drives that were caught, and retired 14 on ground balls.

Herb Carneal

It was the worst feeling I have ever had in my lifetime. I almost took myself out after that inning. I understand how the fans feel. I felt just as bad, maybe worse. He's one of my best friends in baseball.

Dennis Martinez

*Cleveland Indians pitcher,
who unintentionally hit Kirby
Puckett in the face with a
fastball, Sept. 28, 1995*

FAST FACT: The injury initially was thought to bring about the shocking premature retirement of Puckett the following year, though later glaucoma, not the beaning incident, was determined to be the cause.

My most memorable moment as a Twin was that hit.

Paul Molitor

*on his 3000th career hit,
at Kansas City, late in 1996*

Wow, what a performance! He was just unbelievable. He went right at them the whole night. . . . You don't get too many opportunities in the majors to pitch a 1–0 shutout.

Ron Gardenhire

after Johan Santana's complete-game, three-hit masterpiece at Oakland on Aug. 12, 2005. Santana struck out nine A's and at one point retired 20 batters in a row

If you're a baseball fan, that's one of the best ones you'll ever see.

Ozzie Guillen

Chicago White Sox manager, on the Aug. 23, 2005, classic between Chicago and Minnesota, won by the Twins, 1–0, after Jacque Jones broke up White Sox hurler Freddie Garcia's no-hit game with an eighth inning homer. The Twins' Johan Santana, with a three-hit shutout, won the pitching duel over Garcia, who posted a one-hitter

MINNESOTA TWINS ALL-TIME FRANCHISE TEAM

*K*ent Hrbek, Chuck Knoblauch, Sam Rice, Ossie Bluege, Bucky Harris, Paul Molitor, Dan Gladden, Bob Allison, Mickey Vernon, Jim Kaat, Jim Perry, Joe Judge, Greg Gagne . . . and these are guys who didn't make the team!

It only points out the profound talent that the Minnesota Twins (and the Washington Senators before them) have placed on the field through the years. As always, tenure, that reliable benchmark of durability and consistency, merits serious weight against the prodigious marks being put up by today's young players. So, for your scrutinous review and argumentative pleasure: the Minnesota Twins' All-Time Franchise Team.

HARMON KILLEBREW

First base (Wash: 1954–60, Minn: 1961–74)

American League MVP (1969)
AL All-Star (1959, 1961, 1963–71)
five-time AL home-run champion
(1962–64, '67, '69)
Hall of Fame (1984)

⚾ ⚾ ⚾

Being the number-one right-handed home-run hitter in American League history stands out. Being second to Babe Ruth in the American League is quite an honor.

Harmon Killebrew

on two significant career achievements

⚾ ⚾ ⚾

I wasn't the only player who respected Harmon Killebrew. Everyone on our team did. He was our leader. He was a quiet leader, not a rah-rah type. He led by example rather than words.

Danny Thompson

ROD CAREW

Second base (1967–78)

American League Rookie of the Year (1967)
American League MVP (1977)
AL All-Star (1967–78)
Hall of Fame (1991)

The bat was like a magic wand in Rod Carew's hands. . . . Both the left- and right-field gaps were his prey. . . . He smacked the baseball inside the park like it was his personal pinball machine.

Dean Urdahl

Rod Carew's biggest highlight in a Twins uniform occurred on Jersey Day, June 26, 1977. In his honor every jersey given to the fans bore his No. 29. A crowd of 46,463 saw him go 4-for-5, including a homer, and raise his average to .403. His season-ending average of .388 was baseball's best since 1957, when Ted Williams also hit .388.

Dave Mona
Dave Jarzyna

GARY GAETTI
Third base (1981–90)
Two-time AL All-Star (1988, '89)
Gold Glove Award (1986–89)

⚾ ⚾ ⚾

Gary Gaetti became the first player to ever hit two home runs in his first two at-bats of postseason play. He was the 1987 ALCS Most Valuable Player, batting .300.

Dean Urdahl

⚾ ⚾ ⚾

It's right up there with lobster.

Gary Gaetti

on his selection to the 1988 AL All-Star team

ZOILO VERSALLES

Shortstop (Wash: 1959–60, Minn: 1961–67)

American League MVP (1965)
AL All-Star (1963, '65)
Gold Glove Award (1963, '65)

He did everything a team could expect of a leadoff hitter. I don't think I ever saw anyone cover so much ground at shortstop, although he could fumble an easy grounder or hurry a throw. Sometimes he liked to add a little bit of show to a play. In 1965, Zoilo was voted the American League's Most Valuable Player, the first Twin—and still one of only three—ever to receive the honor.

Herb Carneal

Certainly the leader of the Twins was Zoilo Versalles. Zoilo was brilliant at the plate in the leadoff position. Any team with a leadoff man having Zoilo's statistics is going to score a huge quantity of runs.

Bill Morlock
Rick Little
authors

EARL BATTEY

Catcher (Wash: 1960, Minn: 1961–67)

AL All-Star (1962–63, 1965–66)

Gold Glove Award (1961–62)

⚾ ⚾ ⚾

With Battey's arrival, fans in the Upper Midwest were treated to the best all-around catcher in Twins history. Earl moved like a cat behind the plate. His lightning quick throwing release gunned down attempted base-stealers and picked off many who wandered too far off base.

Dean Urdahl

⚾ ⚾ ⚾

Earl Battey was one of the finest catchers I have ever seen. I don't think we realized how great he was until a little after our game. He had a great arm and great knowledge of how to handle pitchers, particularly young pitchers.

Harmon Killebrew

GOOSE GOSLIN

Left field (Wash: 1921–30, 1933, 1938)
Hall of Fame (1968)

American League batting champion (1928)
only man to play in each of the Washington
Senators' 19 World Series games

They oohed and ah'd at the power in his throwing arm and chortled when the Goose threw runners out from deep left and right. But it was at bat that they loved Goslin and the plate-crowding stance he took before fastening a murderous glare on the luckless pitcher of the moment. They knew the power in his big frame, and when he struck out their disappointment was tempered by the gusto of his swing and the massive pirouette that was much like Ruth's.

Shirley Povich

I wouldn't trade Goose Goslin for the whole Yankee Stadium. And I mean it.

Clark Griffith
*manager (1912–20)/
owner (1912–55)*

KIRBY PUCKETT

Center field (1984–95)

AL All-Star (1986–95)

Gold Glove Award (1986–89, 1991–92)

Hall of Fame (2001)

⚾ ⚾ ⚾

When Kirby Puckett retired following the 1995 season, he had attained the highest career batting average (.318) for a right-handed batter since Joe DiMaggio.

National Baseball Hall of Fame

Cooperstown, N.Y.

⚾ ⚾ ⚾

I don't know how many at-bats he had, but I know that for three-quarters of them I was standing in the on-deck circle watching him hit. I don't know how many times I'd walk up to the plate, and the catcher would be sitting there shaking his head, going, "Can't believe he hit that pitch" or "How do you get this guy out?"

Kent Hrbek

on Kirby Puckett

TONY OLIVA

Right field (1962–76)

AL Rookie of the Year (1964)
AL All-Star (1964–71)
Sporting News AL Player of the Year (1965, '71)
Gold Glove Award (1966)

Tony Oliva belongs in the Hall of Fame. He was the toughest hitter I faced; ask any right-handed pitcher.

Dean Chance

FAST FACT: In addition to hurling three seasons with Minnesota, Chance faced Oliva as a pitcher for the L.A./California Angels, Cleveland Indians, and Detroit Tigers.

When asked what honor he most valued, Tony didn't mention the three batting titles or being named to the All-Star Game his first six seasons. Instead, Oliva cited the Gold Glove he won for his fielding in 1966. By his own admission, he started as a poor outfielder and worked hard to improve. It paid off.

Dean Urdahl

WALTER JOHNSON

Pitcher (Wash: 1907–27)

American League MVP (1913, '24)
12-time AL strikeout king
five-time AL ERA leader
two-time 30-game winner
Hall of Fame (1936)

The first time I faced him I watched him take that easy windup, and then something went past that made me flinch. The thing just hissed with danger. [It was] the most threatening sight I ever saw on a ball field. We couldn't touch him . . . every one of us knew we'd met the most powerful arm ever turned loose in a ballpark.

Ty Cobb
on Walter Johnson's major-league debut against Detroit, Aug. 2, 1907

TOM KELLY

Manager (1986–2001)

winningest manager in Twins history (1,140)
AL Manager of the Year (1991)

When you give Tom Kelly players with the ability to compete, his managerial skills are second to none on the field. He's never gotten the accolades he deserves, even though he won two World Series, because he manages a midwestern team in a small market.

Gene Larkin

I wanted the opportunity to play for Tom Kelly. He was very sharp on the field and was never outmatched. His match-ups are always the way he wants them. . . . He knows the game; he understands it. T.K.'s biggest attribute is that he wants the players to play the game. He encourages the players to keep him out of it.

Terry Steinbach

Minnesota Twins All-Time Franchise Team

Harmon Killebrew, *first base*

Rod Carew, *second base*

Gary Gaetti, *third base*

Zoilo Versalles, *shortstop*

Earl Battey, *catcher*

Goose Goslin, *left field*

Kirby Puckett, *center field*

Tony Oliva, *right field*

Walter Johnson, *pitcher*

Tom Kelly, *manager*

THE GREAT TWINS TEAMS

We lost 22 games in spring training. It was great to see it all come together. We were positive we could win each game. The chemistry of that team became a life lesson to me. I don't remember the hits. I remember the ultimate team game.

Rich Rollins

on the 1965 American League-champion Twins

In 1962, my first season with Minnesota, after a record of 70–90 the year before, the Twins were in close contention with the New York Yankees and finished the year in second place, only five games out of first, with a record of 91–71. It was only the second winning season for the franchise since the end of World War II. Every other car on the road had a "Win Twins!" bumper sticker.

Herb Carneal

The 1965 team had excellent pitching and a power-laden lineup. Ironically, two of the team's stars had off seasons due to injuries. Camilo Pascual won just nine games, and Harmon Killebrew hit only 25 home runs—still respectable seasons but definite drop-offs from their previous years.

Dean Urdahl

We got in the lead early, and we never relinquished it. We just pulled together, and it was a great relationship with each player. You're more friends when you win, anyway, and we won the whole year. We had a great time.

Al Worthington
pitcher (1964–69),
on the '65 Twins

The Twins teams of 1969 and '70 were perhaps the finest blend of hitting, defense, and pitching in Minnesota history. They were a collection of talented players that featured two future Hall of Fame inductees, Harmon Killebrew and Rod Carew, and other viable Hall candidates like Jim Kaat, Bert Blyleven, and Tony Oliva. They also had two Cy Young Award winners: Dean Chance from 1964 and Jim Perry from 1970.

Dean Urdahl

There wouldn't be enough money for a franchise to pay that team today.

Jim Perry
*pitcher (1963–72),
on the 1969 and '70 Twins teams*

I haven't been in the clubhouse since 1941, but I wanted to come in here tonight to tell you I believe we have the best team we've had in the past four years. I believe we can win the pennant. The next time I come into a clubhouse, it's going to be to drink champagne with you.

Calvin Griffith

prior to the opening game of 1975

The Twins emerged as definite contenders in the American League West, going into the last week of the season before being eliminated.

Dave Mona
Dave Jarzyna

on the 1984 Twins

We were the worst team in the world in '82 and to go from there and get to here . . . to go through what we went through and finally win it . . .

Randy Bush

on the '87 team

FAST FACT: Bush was part of a small group of players that lost 102 games in 1982, including 46 of 55 games during one stretch.

What kind of team was the Twins? It was a team of big eaters and big hitters. A little like the slow-pitch softball team that won the Rec League championship.

Doug Grow

on the 1987 world-champion Twins

We always won when we had to win. That's what I'll remember about this year.

Steve Lombardozzi

on the 1987 Twins

The 1987 Minnesota Twins become the first team in the history of baseball to go into the World Series having been outscored, out-hit, out-homered, and out-pitched in terms of earned-run average. They were out-everythinged! Except at this point, there are 13 teams in the American League that are out of the World Series, and the Minnesota Twins are in it.

Al Michaels

⚾ ⚾ ⚾

Kelly's team had won 103 games in anger and had clearly proven to be the best in baseball.

Ted Robinson
on the 1991 world champions

⚾ ⚾ ⚾

I don't mind wanting our team to play like the Twins do. I'm impressed with how they win. They make few mistakes.

Alan Trammell
former Detroit Tigers manager, on the 2005 Minnesota Twins

These 2005 Minnesota Twins apparently aren't Luke Skywalker's kind of team. Or B. B. King's kind of team. They'd never be caught reading *Ball Four*. And they'll never take a stroll down anyone's Walk of Fame. In a sport where way too many pitchers can't tell the strike zone from a time zone, these 2005 Twins have turned into an entire pitching staff of control freaks. Any time you find yourself comparing a team to the 1876 Hartford Dark Blues and the 1906 White Sox, you know you're talking about a team that is, officially, from a whole 'nother era. But that's where these Twins find themselves these days, throwing strikes at a rate that's unheard of in the 21st century.

Jayson Stark
ESPN.com

11

FIELDS OF PLAY

Metropolitan Stadium was built on 164 acres in the middle of a cornfield. The stadium looked like the product of a spoiled child's Erector Set. It had a crazy-quilt combination of triple-decked, double-decked, and single-decked stands, with no roofs over any of them.

Lawrence S. Ritter

author

Jimmy Manning went ahead and built his new park on Florida Avenue and named it American League Park. Once more a brand-new team of Washington Senators opened a brand-new season in a brand-new park under brand-new ownership and a brand-new manager.

Morris A. Bealle

on D.C.'s newest ballpark, 1901

The first act of the new ownership was to move back to old National Park at Seventh and Florida Avenue.

Morris A. Bealle

*on the 1904 Senators under
new management headed by
William J. Dwyer*

FAST FACT: For clarification: Both American League Park and National Park were located on Florida Avenue. The Nationals played in American League Park from 1901 through '03 and in National Park from 1904 through '60. Just before the 1911 season, fire destroyed the grandstand and bleachers, but by opening day, enough of the park had been rebuilt so that continuous play there was not interrupted. By midseason a new concrete and steel structure had replaced most of the original park. The facility was renamed Griffith Stadium, after owner Clark Griffith, in 1920.

Legend has it that it was downhill, and only 89 feet, from the plate to first base in Griffith Stadium, supposedly to help save a step for slow Washington batters.

Philip J. Lowry
author

⚾ ⚾ ⚾

Griffith Stadium was a difficult park in which to hit home runs. The original (1911) dimensions were 407 feet from home plate down the left-field line, 421 feet to center field, and 320 feet down the right-field line. A 30-foot-high concrete wall dominated right field, and balls hitting it were in play. . . . On April 17, 1953, Yankee outfielder Mickey Mantle, batting right-handed, hit a gargantuan home run off Washington left-hander Chuck Stobbs that cleared the left-field wall and landed a guesstimated 565 feet from home plate.

Lawrence S. Ritter

The center-field wall in Griffith Stadium detoured around five houses and a huge tree in center, jutting into the field of play.

Philip J. Lowry

In the summer of 1932, he sold hot dogs for a dime and dispensed Coke from ice buckets. The hot dogs were big movers, considering it was the Depression. The Coke was an easy nickel, too, but the empty bottles too often became weapons to be used in the impromptu riots that flared up in the bleachers. Daniels witnessed the introduction of paper cups.

Joe Soucheray

author,
on longtime Senators/Twins
commissary supervisor Charles
Daniels's humble beginnings as a
food hawker at Griffith Stadium

Fortress on the Prairie.

Anonymous visiting writer

on Metropolitan Stadium, home to the Minnesota Twins from 1961 through '81

You not only built a stadium, but one of the finest in the country. You ask if this compares with the major leagues. It's as good as any and better than most of them.

Horace Stoneham

onetime owner of the New York/ San Francisco Giants and an opening-day visitor to Metropolitan Stadium on April 24, 1956. A group attempting to bring major-league baseball to Minnesota had courted the Giants' owner in hopes he would relocate the club to the Twin Cities

This was the second major-league park built in a cornfield. . . . It was by far the most poorly maintained ballpark in the Majors. In 1981, broken railings on the third deck overlooking the left-field bleachers created a safety hazard. When the Hubert H. Humphrey Metrodome was finished, the Met became the first modern stadium to be abandoned.

Philip J. Lowry

Metropolitan Stadium was the home of the Minnesota Twins for their first 21 seasons. In those 21 years, it was the site of an All-Star Game, a World Series, and two American League Championship Series.

Dave Mona
Dave Jarzyna

FAST FACT: The Met was constructed in 1955.

I can close my eyes and see a lot of Killebrew home runs in that park. Those are my best memories.

Calvin Griffith
on Metropolitan Stadium

Much of the Met's character had to do with the fact that it wasn't perfect. The bleachers in left didn't match the bleachers in right, and the folding chairs along the left-field line didn't match anything. The Met also had grass, and its old-fashioned non-computerized scoreboard featured the Twins-O-Gram, the stadium message board that is probably best remembered for reporting the distances of home runs.

Dave Mona
Dave Jarzyna

Metropolitan Stadium

Everyone started referring to the new left-field wall at Metropolitan Stadium as Borgie's Porch. The wall was built from the left-field foul line to center field. It used to be 346 feet down the left-field line; now it's only 330. More important, it was 365 feet to left-center field, the power alley; now it's only 346. . . . No one was as confident as our catcher, Glenn Borgmann, that the new wall would increase his home-run total. We accuse Glenn of having "warning track power" because he can hit a ball to any track in the league. It wouldn't matter if that wall was two hundred or five hundred feet away, he'd still only reach the warning track. That's when we started calling the wall Borgie's Porch.

Danny Thompson

The Met is a ballpark with all the wonder and excitement the name implies. The real shame of shifting our games indoors does not lie so much with the loss of the Met as it does with the loss of games played outdoors.

Joe Soucheray

They told me to move downtown or get out of town.

Calvin Griffith

on his waffling stance in the late 1970s between wanting to remodel Metropolitan Stadium or supporting the downtown domed-stadium project (Hubert H. Humphrey Metrodome)

We need a domed stadium. Every player on our club believes that. Early in the season and also in September, the weather is so unpredictable that many fans won't risk coming to the stadium because the game might be postponed. With a dome, they wouldn't have that problem.

Danny Thompson

For many fans, the end of the Metropolitan Stadium was like losing a friend.

Herb Carneal

When the end came, it came quickly, on a cold rainy day on Sept. 30, 1981, before a small crowd of the Met's old friends. Each fan was given a certificate of attendance, and those coming just for the baseball were sorely disappointed, because the Twins lost to Kansas City.

Dave Mona
Dave Jarzyna

It is cold and gray and impersonal, a little bit of gloom even on the cheeriest summer day. It has no flowerbeds, no flagstone walks, no three-season porch, no fireplace to cozy up to. No southern exposure, no western exposure, no exposure, period, beyond perhaps indecent. Its décor is early mausoleum, its color scheme splashed on from whatever was left of PT 109. Dorothy and Toto would have turned and headed straight back to Oz. Thomas Wolfe wouldn't even have tried to go back there. But to the Twins, the Hubert H. Humphrey Metrodome is home. Home sweet home. Or rather, dome sweet dome.

Steve Aschburner

Baseball fans in the Upper Midwest were curious about this new inflatable ballpark that had opened in downtown Minneapolis. On April 6, 1982, 52,279 customers witnessed the first American League game in the Metrodome, an 11–7 Twins loss to Seattle. The attendance was the largest regular-season crowd in the Twins' first 25 years.

Dave Mona
Dave Jarzyna

Classic Dome ball is what it was. Rock music, line drives, and screaming fans. . . . Home runs for the hometown team and lost fly balls for the visitors.

Doug Grow
on the Metrodome

It is the only park in baseball besides Boston's venerable Fenway Park in which the outfield fence is a different height in each field.

Steve Aschburner

on the Dome

⚾ ⚾ ⚾

This place just has enough quirks that you have more funny things happen here, and the home team gets used to them. That builds confidence.

Roy Smalley Jr.

*shortstop (1976–82, 1985–87),
on the Metrodome*

⚾ ⚾ ⚾

More than a 727 . . . forget the decibel meter, get the Richter scale! Now we know what sound feels like!

Al Michaels

*on the deafening noise level
inside the Metrodome*

You've got to be physical to watch a game here.

Tim McCarver

on the Metrodome

In early 1984, Dave Kingman of the Oakland A's did something that never had been done. He hit a towering pop-up through one of the drainage holes in the fabric roof of the Metrodome. While Twins [players] and fans waited for the ball to come down, Kingman quietly took his place on second base after being awarded a ground-rule double.

Dave Mona
Dave Jarzyna

With the light-colored dome as a background, a ball can easily get misplaced up there and end up on the ground.

Al Michaels

*on the treacherous sight
conditions, especially for
opponents, in the Metrodome*

I liked the Metrodome. It was fast, kinda sterile for a while, but when the crowds were large, it was awesome. The best home-field advantage ever, with the ceiling and the lights and the baggie. We pretty much adopted it as our favorite place to play. It wasn't a great baseball stadium compared to some that have been built, but it was ours and we took advantage of playing there.

Gary Gaetti

Good things happen here.

Roy Smalley Jr.

on the Metrodome

The play was a disgrace to baseball.

Tony LaRussa

criticizing the playing surface at the Metrodome after his Chicago White Sox lost to Minnesota, 3–2, in June 1984 on a bizarre play involving the stadium's artificial surface. With two runners on, Twins batter Tim Teufel's hit to short-right field turned into an inside-the-park home run when the ball apparently hit a seam and bounced crazily over Sox right fielder Harold Baines's head all the way to the wall

Suggesting that all we need at the Metrodome is more innovative noise is like saying all the Atlantic Ocean needs is more water.

Jim Klobuchar

Minnesota's pro teams will begin playing games in the Hubert H. Humphrey Metrodome downtown in the spring of 1982. Speaking for the vast assemblage of fans largely helpless to this inevitability, I could not be more displeased if our lakes were to be ruined with clean fill and converted into subdivisions.

Joe Soucheray

Somewhere in the vibrating membranes of the Metrodome roof, they put engineers to work measuring the sound in the 1987 World Series. The needle ran up against the red line when Dan Gladden hit that bases-loaded home run on opening night. The engineers said it produced 118 decibels of din. That was comparable to a jet airliner taking off in the next lane.

Jim Klobuchar

THE FANS

Nothing will ever match, for me, the emotions of the 1987 crowds.

Tom Kelly

The Washington fans stand, and have stood for 80 years, in a class by themselves. No other fandom in the world can even attempt to approach them for loyalty, patience, and the ability to take incredible mental punishment.

Morris A. Bealle

1947

The nation's capital, inured to the excitement of presidential inaugurations, calm in the midst of history-making legislation, and calloused to the fetes for visiting princes and potentates, went wild on Oct. 1, 1924, and exploded emotionally.

Shirley Povich

on Washington fans' reaction to the Senators' first-ever American League pennant, following Washington's 5–3 victory over Boston coupled with a Yankees loss to the Philadelphia Athletics

When Bucky Harris and his Senators detrained at Union Station, the city's first pennant clinched, they were swept up in a whirl of giddily happy fans. Total strangers pounded each other on the back. Storekeepers vied in dressing their show windows with baseball paraphernalia. Songs of Harris and the team mushroomed in the night clubs, and countless thousands lined Pennsylvania Avenue for the victory parade.

Shirley Povich

*on the pageantry surrounding
the Senators' American League
championship in 1924*

I think I'm a person who looked out for the fan. I think I was always honest with them. I don't lie. . . . We made mistakes. But my mind has always been open for the betterment of baseball.

Calvin Griffith

There were "Bring Billy Back" bumper stickers all over town, and a lot of fans vowed they would never go to another Twins game. Every so often in later years, I heard from people who said they hadn't been back since Martin was fired.

Herb Carneal

on the fallout of Calvin Griffith's firing of the popular Minnesota manager following the 1969 season

The fans were really great. I've been hung in apathy before so I didn't know what to expect.

Calvin Griffith

It looks like about 46,000 people are going to miss this game.

Rod Carew

on the April 16, 1975, turnout of 2,262 at Metropolitan Stadium for the game against California

I would say that 90 percent of our fans for 15 years came to cheer Harmon Killebrew. The rural people all felt close to him. He was a symbol. A big sturdy man who seemed basically simple and fond of the ordinary things—kind of a true man of the West. . . . When he flexed his muscles at the plate it was like all of our small-town and farmer friends were up there swinging with him.

Anonymous small-town mayor in Minnesota

Fans will start to support us, if the weather warms up—and if we win.

Danny Thompson
April 1975

Those first few years at the Met were paradise. We got big crowds all the time. Everybody was so goldarn happy. . . . I got a license plate that said "Twins," and people would drive by me, honking their horns and smiling and waving. Not like later on, when they'd give me the finger.

Calvin Griffith

Upwards of a quarter-million people lined the streets of the Twin Cities to cheer on the Twins in a wild celebration that concluded at the state capitol.

Bob Costas

on the aftermath of Minnesota's
1987 World Series triumph

Men cried and, as they did, their fans cheered. That's special, and that was the highlight of the Twins' 1987 season.

Jay Weiner

People in the Upper Midwest always have been wise enough not to take their sports too seriously. They've always been wise enough to know that it sometimes makes more sense to go fishing than go to the ballpark. But they also were wise enough to take a month-long holiday from reality.

Doug Grow

referring to the Twins' magical month of October 1987

It is obvious, as fans of teams, you can no longer identify with the roster, inasmuch as free agency moves players every year. The owners and the players had better come together on some mutual ground. Free agency has gone too far. We have lost the loyalty of the fans to our teams.

Rich Reese

Thing that I remember most from the '87 season was the way most of the people here were screaming, the fans. When the guys from St. Louis kept telling me, "I can't hear! I can't hear!" Well, I couldn't hear either! Nobody could hear. The fans were screaming like crazy. I mean, my ears actually rung, I'm telling you, for like a week.

Kirby Puckett
on the World Series din
at the Dome

It was the fans who gave me the thrills.

Dave Boswell

Usually after a ballgame, you don't hear the fans from the locker room. But it was so loud out there that we could hear them in the locker room. I remember looking at Puck and saying, "Puck, I can't stand it in this locker room. I'm going back outside." Five to 10 minutes later he comes walking out again, and that place went crazy, that place went nuts. I'll never forget that sound. That sound was the most powerful sound I ever heard in a stadium, and it was a bigger roar than when we won Game Seven.

Chili Davis

in the aftermath of Kirby Puckett's game-winning, 11th-inning home run in the Metrodome that beat the Atlanta Braves and forced a Game Seven in the 1991 World Series

We have terrific, noisy crowds. But this one is unreal. It blows me away. I've got an earache and a headache, and I came with radio phones. I'm shook.

Don Sandler

St. Louis Cardinals fan,
at the Metrodome for Game One
of the 1987 World Series

It was the biggest and loudest and most believing revival meeting in the history of Minnesota, and never mind that the organ played rock instead of "Bringin' in the Sheaves."

Jim Klobuchar

during the Twins' 10–1 opening-
game victory over St. Louis in
the 1987 World Series

13

THE
LOCKER ROOM

I've invested too many bats, balls, and gloves in you. You're going back to school. And you're gonna make it!

Kirby Puckett's mom

to young Kirby, then a student-athlete at Bradley University, home on a month-long hiatus due to the death of his father. Puckett assumed he would not be returning to college, that he'd have to look for a job to help out his mom

Ten Senators players had to sleep in the dressing room of Griffith Stadium in April and May 1946 due to a post-war housing shortage.

Philip J. Lowry

⚾ ⚾ ⚾

For the last two years I have been told to go on and do my best and to look ahead to the next year for a big contract. Now I have come to the end of that, and I want to see the money. I have got to get it now, if ever. If I am as good an asset to the club as claimed, I ought to realize something on my value.

Walter Johnson

*pitcher (1907–27),
who held out for $7,000 after
being offered $6,000 by the
Senators for the 1911 season*

Twice Earl Battey suffered broken cheekbones from pitches. Once he was hospitalized after a beaning. After those facial injuries, Earl and Twins' trainer Doc (George) Lentz created the first protective-flap batting helmet, which Battey wore to ward off more damage.

Dean Urdahl

⚾ ⚾ ⚾

I was happy to pitch 25 seasons in the majors, which, when my career ended, was a record. Tommy John eventually pitched in 26 seasons and Nolan Ryan in 27!

Jim Kaat

⚾ ⚾ ⚾

Without baseball, I would have stayed in Cuba and been a farmer, maybe played amateur ball and coached. I wouldn't have met my wife or had my family.

Tony Oliva

I never dreamed I would be playing at the premier level of baseball for so long. Baseball players are great today, but I believe that it doesn't matter what era you're in. If you were a good pitcher, you could pitch now and then.

Camilo Pascual
pitcher (Wash: 1954–60; Minn: 1961–66)

⚾ ⚾ ⚾

In some games he'll play super—make plays no one else can, steal bases with ease, hit the ball all over the park. It's unbelievable how much ability he has. Yet, he doesn't give 100 percent every day, and that upsets the other 24 guys who are trying hard but have less talent. That's the way Rod is.

Danny Thompson
on Rod Carew

The money has obviously changed. The respect for the game has changed. I cannot fathom, the way I grew up, that players make all this money and yet they have to be paid for autographs. They don't continue to build the fan base.

Rich Reese

In the 1970s you didn't talk to the opposing players before the game. Baseball was war, and we were taught to dislike the enemy. Teams mostly developed their own players, and they came up through the system. Free agency changed that. The loyalty players had to one team and one group of players changed.

Bert Blyleven

A lot of fans in Minnesota were bitter because they thought that Jack Morris, a Minnesota native, was being disloyal and going elsewhere just because another team was offering more money. But Twins fans should be thankful for what he did while he was here. The Twins would not have become world champions without him.

Herb Carneal

They had to keep their money for Kirby Puckett, and the team fell apart because of it. But that's business in baseball. I did what I had to do for my future. The Twins did what they felt was right for the community and the popularity of one player.

Jack Morris

on his decision to move on to Toronto after his one glorious season in Minnesota (1991)

My Baby Waves The Homer Hanky."

**Song celebrating the Twins'
1987 championship season**

*(to the tune of "My Baby Does the
Hanky Panky")*

⚾ ⚾ ⚾

Danny Thompson kept playing even after he was diagnosed with leukemia a couple years later. In 1976, the Twins traded him to the Texas Rangers, and at the end of that season Danny died. He was just 29.

Herb Carneal

⚾ ⚾ ⚾

Roy Smalley Jr. and Joe Niekro came to the Twins in 1987 for a price tag of $10 each.

Jack Clary

Walter Johnson's final major-league appearance came as a pinch hitter in the same game in which Babe Ruth hit his then-record 60th home run of the season, Sept. 30, 1927.

National Baseball Hall of Fame

⚾ ⚾ ⚾

Don't feel sad. I got to play the game that I loved and enjoyed so much for 30 years. For years I got to experience what I wanted to do as a kid. How many people can say that?

Kirby Puckett

following his career-ending eye surgery in the summer of 1995

14

WORLD CHAMPION ROSTERS

Sixty-seven years passed between World Series Game Sevens that went into extra innings. How odd that the same franchise produced victories in both: the 1924 Washington Senators and the 1991 Minnesota Twins. A further peculiarity: If a Mr. October were to be selected from each of those classic Series, it would be hard to argue the choice of pitchers—the great Walter Johnson, whose sterling relief effort overcame the New York Giants in '24, and Jack Morris, whose artful 10-inning shutout toppled the Atlanta Braves in '91.

1924 Washington Senators
92–62

World Series victors over New York Giants, 4–3
Stanley "Bucky" Harris, *manager*

Nick Altrock, *pitcher*

Ossie Bluege, *third base*

Carl East, *outfield*

George "Showboat" Fisher, *outfield*

Harold "Chick" Gagnon, *shortstop*

Leon "Goose" Goslin, *left field*

Bert Griffith, *outfield*

William "Pinky" Hargrave, *catcher*

Bucky Harris, *second base*

Walter Johnson, *pitcher*

Joe Judge, *first base*

Wade Lefler, *outfield*

Nemo Leibold, *center field*

Fredrick "Firpo" Marberry, *pitcher*

Joe Martina, *pitcher*

Wid Matthews, *outfield*

Walter "Slim" McGrew, *pitcher*

Earl McNeely, *outfield*

Ralph Miller, *second base*

George Mogridge, *pitcher*

Warren "Curly" Ogden, *pitcher*

Roger Peckinpaugh, *shortstop*

James "Doc" Prothro, *third base*

Edgar "Sam" Rice, *right field*

Lance Richbourg, *outfield*

Herold "Muddy" Ruel, *catcher*

Allan "Rubberarm" Russell, *pitcher*

Ernest "Mule" Shirley, *first base*

Carr Smith, *outfield*

By Speece, *pitcher*

Bennie Tate, *catcher*

Tommy Taylor, *third base*

Frederick "Ted" Wingfield, *pitcher*

Tom Zachary, *pitcher*

Paul Zahniser, *pitcher*

Starters in bold

1987 Minnesota Twins
85–77
World Series victors over St. Louis Cardinals, 4–3
Tom Kelly, *manager*

Keith Atherton,
pitcher

Juan Berenguer,
pitcher

Bert Blyleven,
pitcher

Tom Brunansky,
right field

Randy Bush,
outfield

Mark Davidson,
outfield/DH

George Frazier,
pitcher

Gary Gaetti,
third base

Greg Gagne,
shortstop

Dan Gladden,
left field

Kent Hrbek,
first base

Gene Larkin,
DH/first base/outfield

Tim Laudner,
catcher

Steve Lombardozzi,
second base

Al Newman,
infielder

Joe Niekro,
pitcher

Kirby Puckett,
center field

Jeff Reardon,
pitcher

Roy Smalley Jr.,
designated hitter

Mike Smithson,
pitcher

Les Straker,
pitcher

Frank Viola,
pitcher

1991 Minnesota Twins
95–67
World Series victors over Atlanta Braves, 4–3
Tom Kelly, *manager*

Paul Abbott, *pitcher*

Rick Aguilera, *pitcher*

Allan Anderson,
pitcher

Steve Bedrosian,
pitcher

Randy Bush, *outfield*

Carmen Castillo,
outfield

Charles "Chili" Davis,
designated hitter

Scott Erickson,
pitcher

Greg Gagne,
shortstop

Dan Gladden,
left field

Mark Guthrie, *pitcher*

Brian Harper,
catcher

Kent Hrbek,
first base

Chuck Knoblauch,
second base

Gene Larkin,
outfield

Terry Leach, *pitcher*

Scott Leius,
third base/shortstop

Shane Mack,
right field

Jack Morris, *pitcher*

Pedro Munoz, *outfield*

Al Newman,
shortstop/second base

Junior Ortiz, *catcher*

Mike Pagliarulo,
third base

Kirby Puckett,
center field

Kevin Tapani, *pitcher*

David West, *pitcher*

Carl Willis, *pitcher*

BIBLIOGRAPHY

Aschburner, Steve. "Home sweet Dome." *Magic: The 1987 Twins' Enchanted Season*. Minneapolis-St. Paul, Minn.: Star Tribune, 1987: 24–26.

Aschburner, Steve. "Twins' defense wins games." *Magic: The 1987 Twins' Enchanted Season*. Minneapolis-St. Paul, Minn.: Star Tribune, 1987: 31.

Astor, Gerald. "New Frontiers." *The Baseball Hall of Fame 50th Anniversary Book*. New York: Prentice Hall Press, 1988.

Barreiro, Dan. "The Class of '82 graduates." *Magic: The 1987 Twins' Enchanted Season*. Minneapolis-St. Paul, Minn.: Star Tribune, 1987: 46, 48.

Barreiro, Dan. "Hits, pitching, defense and a crowd that roars." *Magic: The 1987 Twins' Enchanted Season*. Minneapolis-St. Paul, Minn.: Star Tribune, 1987: 64.

Bealle, Morris A. *The Washington Senators: An 87-Year History of the World's Oldest Baseball Club and Most Incurable Fandom*. Washington, D.C.: Columbia Publishing Co., 1947.

Brackin, Dennis. "Sleep's elusive, but not dreams." *Magic: The 1987 Twins' Enchanted Season*. Minneapolis-St. Paul, Minn.: Star Tribune, 1987: 34.

Browning, Reed. *Baseball's Greatest Season: 1924*. Amherst and Boston: University of Massachusetts Press, 2003.

Carew, Rod with Ira Berkow. *Carew*. New York: Simon and Schuster, 1979.

Carlson, Chuck. *Puck! Kirby Puckett: Baseball's Last Warrior*. Lenexa, Kan.: Addax Publishing Group, 1997.

Carneal, Herb with Stew Thornley. *Hi Everybody!* Minneapolis, Minn.: Nodin Press, 1996.

Clary, Jack. *World Champion Minnesota Twins Trivia*. Boston: Quinlan Press, 1987.

Cullum Dick. "The First. The Longest. The Best." *Minneapolis Tribune*. Harmon Killebrew. Minneapolis, Minn.

Goethal, Arno. "Killebrew's Memorable Homers." *St. Paul Dispatch*. Harmon Killebrew. Minneapolis, Minn.

Grow, Doug. "24 down-to-earth guys made October heavenly." *Magic: The 1987 Twins' Enchanted Season*. Minneapolis-St. Paul, Minn.: Star Tribune, 1987: 8.

Grow, Doug. "Championship baseball returns to Minnesota." *Magic: The 1987 Twins' Enchanted Season*. Minneapolis-St. Paul, Minn.: Star Tribune, 1987: 58.

Grow, Doug. "Hugs, emotions and the American League pennant." *Magic: The 1987 Twins' Enchanted Season*. Minneapolis-St. Paul, Minn.: Star Tribune, 1987: 75–76.

Grow, Doug. "Twins roll into their first World Series in 22 years." *Magic: The 1987 Twins' Enchanted Season*. Minneapolis-St. Paul, Minn.: Star Tribune, 1987: 80.

Harlin, Sean and Mike Herman, Molly Gallatin, Brad Steil. *Minnesota Twins Record & Information Book, 2005 Baseball Season*. Minneapolis, Minn.: Minnesota Twins Baseball Club, 2005.

Harris, Stanley. *Playing the Game: From Mine Boy to Manager*. New York: Grosset & Dunlap Publishers, 1925.

Hartman, Sid. "Senator discovered Harmon." *Minneapolis Tribune*. Harmon Killebrew. Minneapolis, Minn.

Kelly, Tom and Ted Robinson. *Season of Dreams: The Minnesota Twins' Drive to the 1991 World Championship*. Stillwater, Minn.: Voyageur Press, Inc., 1992.

Kerr, Jon. *Calvin: Baseball's Last Dinosaur, an Authorized Biography*. Wm. C. Brown Publishers, 1990.

Kirby: Living the Dream. Dir. William Pohlad. Narr. Bob Costas. Minnesota Twins, 1996. 60 min.

Klobuchar, Jim. *High & Inside: A Chronicle of 1987's Daze of Autumn, from the Metrodome to Kent Hrbek's Duck Blind*. Stillwater, Minn.: Voyageur Press, 1987.

Lowry, Philip J. *Green Cathedrals*. Reading, Mass.: Addison-Wesley Publishing Co., Inc., 1992.

Mona, Dave and Dave Jarzyna. *Twenty Five Seasons: The First Quarter Century of the Minnesota Twins*. Minneapolis, Minn.: Mona Publications, 1986.

Morlock, Bill and Rick Little. *Split Doubleheader: An Unauthorized History of the Minnesota Twins*. Morick, Inc., 1979.

Nichols, Max. "Harmon Class of Clubhouse." *Minneapolis Star*. Harmon Killebrew. Minneapolis, Minn.

Povich, Shirley. *The Washington Senators*. New York: G. P. Putnam's Sons, 1954.

Riley, Don. "Killebrew: A quiet man." *St. Paul Pioneer Press*. Harmon Killebrew. Minneapolis, Minn.

Ritter, Lawrence S. *Lost Ballparks: A Celebration of Baseball's Legendary Fields*. New York: The Penguin Group, 1992.

Ross, Alan. *Echoes from the Ballpark*. Nashville, Tenn.: Walnut Grove Press, 1999.

Shannon, Bill. *Topps Baseball Cards: Minnesota Twins*. Los Angeles: Price Stern Sloan, Inc., 1989.

Sinker, Howard. "Twins and Puckett soar on opening day." *Magic: The 1987 Twins' Enchanted Season*. Minneapolis-St. Paul, Minn.: Star Tribune, 1987: 16, 17.

Soucheray, Joe. *Once There Was a Ballpark: The Seasons of the Met, 1956–1981*. Edina, Minn.: Dorn Books, 1981.

1987 World Series: There's No Place Like Home. Prod. Major League Baseball Productions and ABC Sports. Narr. Al Michaels. CBS/FOX Video, 1987.

The 1991 World Series: Minnesota Twins vs. Atlanta Braves. Dir. Rich Domich. Narr. Ernie Harwell. Major League Baseball Home Video, 1991. 60 min.

Thompson, Danny with Bob Fowler. *E–6: The Diary of a Major League Shortstop*. Minneapolis, Minn.: Dillon Press, Inc., 1975.

Thorn, John et al. *Total Baseball: The Official Encyclopedia of Major League Baseball*, Fifth Edition. New York: Viking Penguin, 1997.

Urdahl, Dean. *Touching Bases with Our Memories: The Players Who Made the Minnesota Twins, 1961–2001*. St. Cloud, Minn.: North Star Press of St. Cloud, Inc., 2001.

Vancil, Mark. "The magic number is one." *Magic: The 1987 Twins' Enchanted Season*. Minneapolis-St. Paul, Minn.: Star Tribune, 1987: 37.

Vancil, Mark. "The magic number is zero." *Magic: The 1987 Twins' Enchanted Season*. Minneapolis-St. Paul, Minn.: Star Tribune, 1987: 41–43.

Vancil, Mark. "'We played hard, we played real hard'." *Magic: The 1987 Twins' Enchanted Season*. Minneapolis-St. Paul, Minn.: Star Tribune, 1987: 69.

Weiner, Jay. "An enchanted season happens only once." *Magic: The 1987 Twins' Enchanted Season*. Minneapolis-St.

Paul, Minn.: Star Tribune, 1987: 2, 4.

Zgoda, Jerry. "Memorable Moments: February." *Magic: The 1987 Twins' Enchanted Season*. Minneapolis-St. Paul, Minn.: Star Tribune, 1987: 11.

Zgoda, Jerry. "Memorable Moments: June." *Magic: The 1987 Twins' Enchanted Season*. Minneapolis-St. Paul, Minn.: Star Tribune, 1987: 21.

Zgoda, Jerry. "Memorable Moments: August." *Magic: The 1987 Twins' Enchanted Season*. Minneapolis-St. Paul, Minn.: Star Tribune, 1987: 27.

⚾ ⚾ ⚾

WEB SITES

Associated Press. "A-Rod goes 0-for–3 on 30th birthday as Yanks slip in AL East." http://sports.espn.go.com/mlb/recap?gameId=250727110, July 27, 2005.

Associated Press. "Crede drives in winning run with 10th-inning infield single." http://sports.espn.go.com/mlb/recap?gameId=250916109, Sept. 16, 2005.

Associated Press. "Hunter suffered broken ankle, not tendon tear." http://sports.espn.go.com/mlb/news/story?id=2121938, Aug. 2, 2005.

Associated Press. "Jones also had game-winning hit Tuesday." http://sports.espn.go.com/mlb/recap?gameId=250720109, July 20, 2005.

Associated Press. "Jones' game-winner a one-hit wonder for Twins, Santana." http://sports.espn.go.com/mlb/recap?gameId=250823109, Aug. 23, 2005.

Associated Press. "Santana comes through for 15th win of 2005." http://sports.espn.go.com/mlb/recap?gameId=250927109, Sept. 27, 2005.

Associated Press. "Santana extends majors-leading strikeout total to 114." http://sports.espn.go.com/mlb/recap?gameId=250608129, June 8, 2005.

Associated Press. "Santana outduels Haren, fans nine in complete game." http://sports.espn.go.com/mlb/recap?gameId=250812111, Aug. 12, 2005.

Associated Press. "Twins get eighth win in nine games." http://sports.espn.go.com/mlb/recap?gameId=250607129, June 7, 2005.

Associated Press. "Twins score three in 11th to beat

ChiSox." http://sports.espn.go.com/mlb/recap?gameId= 250922104, Sept. 22, 2005.

Associated Press. "White Sox drop seventh of their last nine." http://sports.espn.go.com/mlb/recap?gameId= 250917109, Sept. 17, 2005.

Baseball America Features: "2005 Top 100 Prospects: 1–25." http://www.baseballamerica.com/today/features/040228to p1004.html, March 3, 2005.

Christensen, Joe. "Third-place finish doesn't bother Santana —much." *Star Tribune*. http://www.startribune.com/stories/ 509/5715894.html, Nov. 8, 2005.

Griffith Stadium. Wikipedia. http://en.wikipedia.org/wiki/ Griffith_Stadium.

Harmon Killebrew quotes. Thinkexist.com. http://en.think exist.com/quotes/harmon_killebrew.

Jeffrey Leonard. BaseballLibrary.com. http://www.baseball library.com/baseballlibrary/ballplayers/L/Leonard_Jeffrey .stm.

Joe Mauer Fan Club. http://www.joemauerfanclub.com.

Ken Burns quotes. BrainyQuote.com. http://www.brainyquote .com/quotes/quotes/k/kenburns263376.html.

Kirby Puckett. National Baseball Hall of Fame. http://www.baseballhalloffame.org/hofers_and_honorees/ hofer_bios/Puckett_Kirby.htm.

"Quotations about the Midsummer Classic." Baseball Quotes: From and About. http://www.baseball-almanac.com/ quotes/allstarquot.shtml.

"Quotations from & about Harmon Killebrew." Baseball Quotes: From and About. http://www.baseball-almanac.com/ quotes/quobrew.shtml.

Stark, Jayson. "'Professor Radke' leads by example." ESPN.com. http://sports.espn.go.com/mlb/columns/story? columnist=stark_jayson&id=2088251, June 17, 2005.

Stark, Jayson. "Santana, not Colon, deserved to win AL Cy Young." ESPN.com. http://sports.espn.go.com/mlb/columns/ story?columnist=stark_jayson&id=2217711, Nov. 8, 2005.

The Ballplayers Historical Biographies. "Earl Battey Statistics." Baseball Almanac. http://www.baseball-almanac.com/players/player.php?p=batteea01.

page Two. "Greatest Pitching Feats: Best of the Last 25 Years." ESPN.com. http://sports.espn.go.com, Sept. 16, 2005.

INDEX

Index

Index

Index

Index